£7.50

TEMPUS
Oral History
SERIES

NEW FOREST
voices

A New Forest Living

Brusher Mills, the snake catcher – an old New Forest character who died in 1905. (9C)

TEMPUS
Oral History
SERIES

NEW FOREST
voices

A New Forest Living

Compiled by
Mike Turner

TEMPUS

First published 1999
Copyright © Mike Turner, 1999

Tempus Publishing Limited
The Mill, Brimscombe Port,
Stroud, Gloucestershire, GL5 2QG

ISBN 0 7524 1625 1

Typesetting and origination by
Tempus Publishing Limited
Printed in Great Britain by
Midway Clark Printing, Wiltshire

This book is dedicated to the Commoners of the New Forest

PICTURE ACKNOWLEDGEMENTS

Sources of pictures are abbreviated as follows:
9C: New Forest Ninth Century Trust, New Forest Museum and Leisure Centre,
Lyndhurst.
AB: Allan Brown, from his book *They Flew from the Forest*.
FC: Forestry Commission, The Queen's House, Lyndhurst.
H: The Humby family.
L: St Barbe Museum, New Street, Lymington.
OW: Edward Jewell, Shelley Farm, Ower, Romsey.
PM: Mrs Pauline Maddigan, Lamb Inn, Nomansland.
SN: Southern Newspapers plc.

NB: *Copyright of the pictures remains with the acknowledged suppliers as listed above*

contents

introduction

Although this book consists almost entirely of tape-recorded conversations with people who live or work in the New Forest, it is not only a work of oral history. One of my concerns has been not only to find out what life was like in the past but also to show how the Forest and its people had changed at the time the recordings took place, that is between autumn 1990 and autumn 1991.

What interests me is how people's lives alter as the world around them changes. The Forest area is a very different place now from what it was when I first knew it, fifty years ago. During and just after the war the New Forest was still a wild tract of land not very different from the days when William the Conqueror first recognized what a wonderful place it was and claimed it for his royal hunting ground. Now the area is polka-dotted with car parks. Huge campsites sprawl across the lawns where once only ponies grazed. And in the distance from many parts of the eastern Forest you can always see the silver towers of the Esso oil refinery and the tall stack of Marchwood power station.

For readers who perhaps only know the Forest as a beautiful, unfenced area of woodland and heath, a place for relaxation, exercise and enjoyment, but are not familiar with its thousand-year-old history and organization, the following remarks may be helpful.

The Forest has always been an infertile and uncultivated place. When King William grabbed the area for his private fun-park he cracked down on the few inhabitants; they could no longer kill the game for food (this was redefined as poaching) nor fence in the land to rear a few cattle – because huntsmen hate fences. But they *were* permitted to run their cattle on the unfenced Forest land and were given other rights; of gathering fuel, for instance, or of digging marl, which was used as a fertilizer before the days of ICI. So the modern landscape and the lifestyle of the Commoners were created in the eleventh century and survived in much the same form until the early twentieth.

Surrounding the New Forest common land there are the Estates, enclosed areas of cultivated land which, roughly two hundred years ago, were shaped into park- and farmland for the gentry. Many of these Estates still exist; the Crosthwaite-Eyre Estate in the north and the Pylewell Estate in the south, for instance, together with the more ancient Montagu Estate in the Beaulieu area, which houses the nationally famous Motor Museum, and the now industrialized Cadland Estate.

The changes began after the First World War when the gravel roads were macadamized to accommodate the new motor car. In those early years a car was an unusual sight, especially in the deepest forest. But by the end of the Second World War cars were well on the way to becoming the transport of the common man and woman that we know today. If you have cars, you need petrol, and it was in the late forties that the Waterside – the eastern edge of the Forest bordering Southampton Water – became heavily industrialized through

New Forest beech trees. (9C)

the expansion of the small AGWI oil refinery into the enormous Esso plant with its attendant power station and chemical works. The refinery is on the site of the Cadland Estate and has produced considerable social change in the Forest villages. Many of the Commoners and smallholders went to work in the refinery from 1948 onwards and this social shift is mentioned by some of the people I have spoken to.

The Commoners (i.e. those who, by living within the Forest boundary, have the right to run cattle on the Forest land) had for some time eked out their existence with secondary jobs, but by working at Esso they now had even less time to work on the land. They spent what seems to urban folk an extraordinary amount of time toiling, either at home or on the smallholding,

or on shift work at Esso (and to a lesser extent at Wellworthy's piston factory at Lymington).

By the 1950s, the Forest was in a mess. The cheap car and the rise in living standards meant that many more people were able to visit the area, and they did. There were no camping restrictions or car parks – holidaymakers and day trippers parked anywhere on the heathland or in the woods; they set up their tents, made cooking fires, ate, slept and relieved themselves where they pleased. One of the greatest assets of the Forest is the sense of freedom it gives to the city dweller – and not only to city people. This is often mentioned in the text by Foresters and visitors alike. But by the end of the 1950s, freedom had become anarchy, the heathland was eroded by car tyres and fouled with waste. Something had to be done and during the sixties the car parks were built which now penetrate all areas of the Forest and special sites for campers were set aside.

There was an immediate improvement, but at some cost. Now, no part of the Forest was more than a mile or so from a car park. In the heart of the woodlands, on the tops of the heathland, pet dogs and family saloons were heard and seen. It was, as everybody says, all free.

Other changes were taking place. The Forestry Commission had been reorganized. The planting of conifers was now restricted, so there were fewer clumps of closely planted fir trees with a permanent dusk under their boughs. But the old system of forestry work carried out by local men on their own beats had been replaced by hiring contract labour from outside. However efficient they may be, contract workers do not live and work in one area of one forest and they do not grow to love the place as the old workers did.

But the Forestry Commission is not only a tree-growing concern; it is also a landlord and its new policy of selling Commission-owned cottages at the market rate had a disastrous effect on the Commoners, who could no longer afford the sky-high prices of the 1980s housing market. The blame for this short-sighted policy rests surely with the central government and the determination of politicians in the eighties to run every aspect of British life as if it were a grocer's shop.

And the conservationists arrived. Conservationists are prolific book-writers; their case can easily be found elsewhere. What I have recorded in this book is the rarely heard resentment felt by those who have to make a living from the Forest when their age-old experience and practice have been ignored by conservationists.

In 1987 a report was published – *The New Forest Review* – which is referred to in the text by several speakers. This book, compiled by a committee of experts, identified most of the problems which occur in the New Forest and the dilemmas which confront Forest people. Certain recommendations were made.

Alongside these changes, some things have remained the same. The Forest is still run and ruled by the verderers and agisters in the ancient fashion. The verderers (from the Norman French *vert* = green) are the elected overseers of the Forest. They hold court every two months at the Queen's House, Lyndhurst (also the headquarters of the local section of the Forestry Commission), where any member of the public can make a 'presentment' about New Forest issues. The agisters (from a Norman word meaning 'to receive payment') are the executive arm of the verderers. They check the condition of the Commoners' animals, they run the annual pony round-ups (drifts) and deal with those animals injured by road traffic.

The Commoners also have their own organization, the Commoners' Defence Association (commonly called the CDA), which holds regular meetings in various locations in the New Forest and is well supported by the Commoners. Then there is the County Council, responsible for the roads which run through the Forest. The County Council also looks after other aspects of Forest life which are common to all

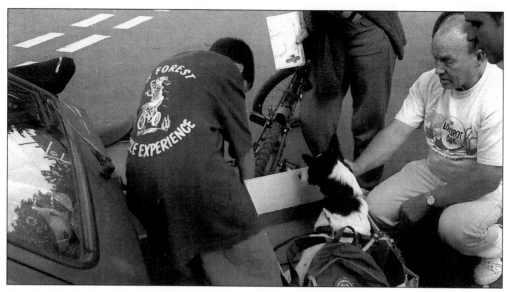

The Forest experience. Cycle hire at Brockenhurst, 1998.

rural areas.

That, briefly, is how the Forest is run. Readers who are interested in finding out more about the administration and control of the New Forest will find plenty of material in the local collections of the Hampshire County Library Service, especially in Southampton Central Library.

I left the Forest area in the sixties and did not return for some fifteen years. Even then, I was no nearer than Southampton, ten miles from the boundary – but I managed to cycle out to the countryside several times a week. From the days when I lived in the Forest I knew that many of my neighbours still lived and worked in the Forest in the old way. Quite often their families had made their homes in New Forest villages for generations. Was it, I wondered, still possible to make a living in the Forest, in spite of the cars, the tourists, the wealthy house buyers and the well-intentioned wildlife enthusiasts?

There was only one way to find out. I dusted off my tape recorder, oiled the chain of my bike and one September evening in 1990 set off from my Southampton home, riding west. This book is the result.

Finally, a note about conventions I have used in the text. Both 'Commoner' and 'Forest' have been capitalized throughout, 'Commoner' to indicate that this is a special class of people when we are talking about the New Forest and 'Forest' when the reference is to the New Forest only. The word 'Estate' when capitalized refers to the landed Estates of the gentry. Villages are close communities and New Forest villages are connected by invisible bonds of kinship and friendship, so in order to disturb this social network as little as possible I have provided everyone with the mask of anonymity except for Ralph Montagu, who is indisguisable, and Sir Dudley Forwood, by his own request.

9

CHAPTER 1
The Working Forest

Cottages at Pilley.

The council flats where Andy lives now.

Andy, Frustrated Commoner

Andy is a former Forestry Commission worker in his thirties and recently married. When I spoke to him he lived temporarily in a farm worker's cottage a couple of miles from the nearest village centre. It is a fine September evening; a New Forest pony grazes on the lawn in front of the house. Andy, his wife and I talk in the darkening living room.

I was working for the Forestry Commission, looking for somewhere to live, to get married. I never had any luck at all with the Forestry Commission. It caused problems, looking for a place and trying to stop them selling houses. I was living at home with my brothers. My father exercised Commoner's rights many years ago, but not sort of on an official basis –

he used to run ponies on the Forest in this area. Our family can be traced back in the New Forest, right back to the seventeen-hundreds, as a travelling family in the Forest – yes, as in gipsies. Most of my family, my relations, still live at Thorney Hill, which is where my father came from. He came from the gipsy camp at Thorney Hill to the gipsy camp which used to be just up the road here, sort of half a mile, in the Forest. It's just a clump of trees in the middle of the Forest which we all know as 'the gipsy camp'. When the gipsies were rehoused, [my family] were rehoused to the cottage where I was born. I'm one of twelve children so we were quite a large family. I'm sort of the outcast of the family. I've gone off and done my own thing.

I've been practising commoning now since I was about fifteen, sixteen. I had

11

my first pony given to me by a local farmer who I used to help. His family had been commoning for years and I used to help him with his ponies, and he said, 'Right, you've got the interest, here's your first pony.' And that's where it all started from and since that I've built up.... It sort of started off with one pony which didn't last very long [he laughs]. Died on me. Then I saved up all my pocket money and bought my first mare when I was sixteen and I've got a family of ponies which I've bred from her. They're all on the Forest now.

You had a bust-up with the Forestry Commission....

Yes. It was more over selling a smallholding. They got my back up. It goes back to a smallholding at Fritham. The Forestry evicted the tenant out of it, who wasn't the tenant – his father used to work for the Forestry Commission – he was evicted on the grounds that he wasn't the tenant. He moved out and the house was left empty for six to eight months. I applied to the Forestry for it and they said, 'Well, we don't know what we're going to do with it. It's Government policy at the moment to sell everything.' So we left it a while and they said they were going to sell it. So we started... just sort of trying to do anything we could find to stop them. We actually stopped them selling it for eighteen months – it was exactly eighteen months to the day they sold it. I even went to the Verderers' Court and stood up and put a presentment up in Court. I went to my local MP, got his backing on it. He done all he could to try and stop it. He even asked questions in the House of Commons on my behalf, but in the end he was just overruled. It was Ministry policy that it was surplus to requirement. I'm not an educated person, but I got letters written all over – New Forest District Council, the Hampshire County Council, the Council for the Protection of Rural England – they all backed me but we were up against more than we could take on. The local branch of the Forestry didn't mind, they were dead against selling it, but we are ruled by Cambridge. Cambridge is the head office of the Forestry Commission for the south-east of England, and they sit in their little office in Cambridge and say, 'Right, that can go, that can go and that can go.' We fought all we could. The house was sold two and a half years ago and it still stands in precisely the same state as the day they sold it, because the New Forest District Council will not give the people who bought it planning permission to pull it down and build a house twice the size, which was thrown out by the planners straight away. And they've just done nothing to it. They're waiting for the house to fall down. Now you can understand why I get riled. [He laughs.]

It even went as far as the Minister for Agriculture. His comment back was 'It has to be sold, it is Government policy. It is surplus to requirements.' And that's the final letter we had back. Six weeks later it was sold at auction for £126,000. It's just pocket money for some people. I couldn't even get the £26,000. I think it's just generally Government policy to flog everything they can. Since I left, they have stopped selling cottages.

George, a New Forest working chap

George is tall, late middle-aged, with nineteenth-century sideburns. We talk in the mess room of his workplace in the old part of Southampton. He is the fastest speaker I met, a continuous stream of stories and reminiscences.

I was born on Blackwell Common, right alongside the Forest. Our old man used to work for Rothies, Rothschild's Estate, for twenty-two years. He used to say, Lionel D. Rothschild – my father's name was Lionel too – Lionel D. Rothschild was a good bloke, but he never had much time for Eddy, that's the son that's there now. He didn't like him. He never liked him at all. Our old man, I mean to say, years ago our old man was a good cricketer down the Exbury club, the old field down there, you know. And our old man was a good cricketer in them days. Rothschild wasn't much good – they put him on because he was the nipper of the old man, the heir or something.

All these kids there – they used to have some parties for them. They used to come round Christmas time and have parties and give kids Christmas presents. We were as poor as church mice. Our old man used to dig a half-acre of ground, look. Keep some pigs. And he used to sell them to old Phil B. in Fawley. He used to slaughter them – the butcher's shop is still there now, in the square. He used to do the slaughtering and everything. Our old man used to have one pig. He used to grow a lot of onions – he was a good gardener, he

George.

used to go in for shows and that. That's the only hobby they had in them days, those sort of people, look. He might go to Exbury Club, but couldn't afford no more, never had no money.

I remember one time the old man – Sandy Nicholas down Exbury, Sandy's brother Sam and my father – they went fishing. They got wet through and the following day Sam Nicholas took my father to Salisbury on a motorbike and they got wet through again. Sam Nicholas died of double pneumonia and the old man didn't, but he did have double pneumonia and he went into hospital and I think he had diseased ribs or something, I forget the name. He was took to Hythe and my father was telling me they couldn't get hold of an anaesthetic in them days. How they

George and his sister.

done the job God knows, because in them days they used to rip them up the sides and put the pipe in, didn't they, in the lung. That's what they used to do in them days, for pneumonia. How they kept him under I don't know. See, there was no anaesthetist in them days, they couldn't get hold of one. For three weeks, my mother was telling me, my father used to have to go to Hythe every day and they used to leave the wound open in them days, and what they used to do was dip the lint in the old iodine and put that in the wound. Used to come home bloody crying. She's dead now, about ten year ago. She was telling me about that. They was cruel bastards in them days, I can tell you that.

Margery, a Commoner who picked it up as she went along

A smallholding/house (the two merge). We talk in a room where every horizontal surface is filled – with papers, magazines and useful items. After a lunch of home-made bread and honey we talk by the window which looks out over the Forest heath.

I married a Manchester man and we lived in suburbia and then we decided to move down here about twenty-seven years ago. He got fed up to the teeth with going ten miles into work – his office was right in the middle of Manchester – and it used to take him an hour to go ten miles and he would be changing gear all the time, in a queue. So he said, 'Where shall we go and live?' – which is a very difficult decision

Margery in her farmyard.

Margery.

Margery, pig beautician.

to make. I thought we'd be a sailing family, because he was handicapped and his family had always sailed – and I wanted to – so we thought we'd come down here; we had some friends down here. We did and sailing didn't seem to take off at all so eventually he came home saying somebody had paid him, or in lieu of payment given him, an eighteen-month-old New Forest pony stallion. He said, 'Where do you sell ponies?' So I said, foolishly, 'Let's see what's involved in keeping a pony.' It all began from there, really. We only had a small garden because we were going to have a boat and sail; and so, this pony, when I'd tamed him (he was very nasty), when I'd tamed him, that's when I learnt about commoning rights, because I hadn't anywhere to put him. I begged and borrowed different patches [of pasturing] and then it was obvious he was going to have to go on the

Forest. He wasn't a stallion then, he'd had his operation.

A stallion on that area was no way going to allow *him* to be on there, so he used to shoo him off miles away, which was very trying because I had two small boys. It was quite a performance finding him and bringing him back home with the dog and the two small boys and then them having a ride and so on.... So I got a pony that had been born and bred locally. It takes a lot to make them go off their square mile patch where they're born and bred. So I got another pony and they palled up, and no sooner had they palled up and we got into a good routine than the first one got run over. I was back with one pony. And so it went on. In the end, I had three run over just as I got them quiet for riding.

There'd been a cow roaming round near us; it was a heifer and the old Forester wouldn't sell her to me. She

16

had a beautiful face; I discovered she was a Jersey. Anyway, eventually the old Forester died and the son appeared one evening and said, 'Here, you wanted to buy her, didn't you?' I think I was walking the dog, and I said, 'Oh yes, she's beautiful, I call her Buttercup.' He said, 'Dad always called her Daisy.' He named his price, which was exactly what I had in my Post Office Savings account, so I said, 'Right,' and he said, 'You'd better take her home.' So I set off up the lane with her on a bit of rope and he said, 'Here, you've forgotten this.' And I didn't realize she'd got the calf – she'd just had a calf – and he was fed up with milking her. That was why he was selling her. So of course I had to have a lesson on milking because I'd never milked a cow. This lad taught me and somebody else, a delightful person. My first time at milking I thought I'd be there for ever. I was getting exhausted and your hands hurt and the cow's not used to you... and then somebody came who used to be in service on one of the farms locally and she'd worked in the dairy and she knew all about it. 'Oh here, you do it like this – no, no, not like that.' She gave me a lesson and after that I just got on with it. I don't do it very well, I don't do it the real, proper way I don't think, but it works.

Percy, village undertaker

A substantial cottage in a typical Forest row, overlooking heathland on one side with fields behind. We talk in a cosy parlour with a log fire burning, welcome warmth on a cold November morning. Percy is shortish, smiling; he is now retired.

Percy and his wife, Ellen.

Percy (driving), at a funeral.

I started this business off in 1956 or '7. I was a carpenter and joiner by trade, which I learnt when I left school. Eventually I started my own business as a builder. I'd always done undertaking, working for other people, and then when we were sitting down one night deciding how we should design our bill-heads we said, 'Well, always done undertaking, let's put "Builder, Decorator and Undertaker" – we might get a job one day.' That's how it started; built it up from there.

Does it take you a long time to make a coffin?

Depends how fast you work. It's a specialized trade. If you've been a carpenter all your life and come to work for me, it's no good me saying to you, 'Get on and make a coffin, here's the sizes.' You wouldn't know how to start. Oh yes, it's quite a specialized job, making coffins. It used to take me half as long as it took a man I employed. I could start making a coffin at seven o'clock in the morning and I could have it finished, ready to go out, when I come in to lunch at one o'clock – providing I had no interruptions. But when I employed men, when we had a job come in I used to go out in the yard in the morning early, seven o'clock, and I'd set out the woodwork, set out a coffin and when the chap come in to work, eight o'clock, I'd say, 'There's a coffin set out, Charley, get on and make that.' I always had to go round after they went home at five o'clock and complete it. Well, they used to stop and have a yarn, then stop and have their lunch. I never used to stop. When I started making a coffin I kept going. I used to shut the

Robert and May, 1930s.

shop door and get on to work. I never used to stop until he was finished; lined and polished and all the lot.

You were always with people who were sad. Did that make you sad?

No. No, because it's something I've done all my life. And death is not sad. Death is the ultimate. That's what we're all on the earth for, to die, to go to something better, isn't it? Depends whether you're a believer or not. I believe there is something better, but I'm not a religious man. I've evolved my own religion through a lifetime. I don't think there's many religions that I haven't dealt with, and I've thought to myself, yeah. So I've evolved my own way of going on, with the basic teachings of the Bible in mind. I curse and swear, I drink, I do all the things

you shouldn't do, but I still... I reckon I leads a reasonable life.

Robert and May, Forest lovers and cyclists

A neat house in Lyndhurst. We speak in a room smelling pleasantly of apple charlotte. A grey November afternoon. On the coffee table are photographs of them both in their cycling days.

Did you work in the village?

May:
Yes, at one period. I worked at the top shop in the fashion trade. Then, after I got married and the children got big enough I went to the Lyndhurst school as a dinner lady. I was there for eleven years and I loved it because we

19

Lyndhurst at the turn of the century. (9C)

May in the 1930s.

Lyndhurst, 1998.

Robert today.

21

had two orphanages the children came to, the Church Home and Dr Barnardo's which was at Bank, at Annesley, the big house. And all the children came to the school, and I was their mum. They were lovely.

You used to do a lot of cycling.

May:
We had a tandem.

Robert:
May wasn't a cyclist. I was born in London. We came down to Southampton because my dad went to sea. I belonged to several cycling clubs and I was out training for a time trial, August 9th, 1936. I was with my friend and as we were going back to Southampton there was this fair by the old police station on the old race course. And of course being young lads we hopped off – blow the training for bikes! We met May and her sister and two other locals there and that was it. And that's how we got May introduced to cycling.

Did you take to cycling?

May:
Yes I did. I loved it. I think it was the happiest days really – well, they are, aren't they, before you take on all the problems and the war came. But we used to go out Sundays, all day. Sometimes I'd be the only girl....

Robert:
You didn't want to wear shorts.

May:
No, I didn't, no. Or cycling shoes – I

thought they were awful. But I soon knew I had to wear the right gear for cycling. And I really did – they were lovely boys. I could go out with... be the only girl as I say, there was never any.... I mean we'd go to Tidworth tattoo and perhaps sleep in a haystack on the way back, still no.... It was so different, wasn't it, then? I don't like going out on my bike very much now, not really. Situated here, wherever you go it's traffic, traffic, and they don't bother about the cyclist at all, do they? Especially this road that they've made into a bypass at Emery Down and it's all potholes and bits of mended bits with holes, so that means you've got to go out in the middle of the road and you're very vulnerable. I think you are. I think it's dreadful. Even to walk along there. We used to take the children along there blackberrying, they could dodge backwards and forwards without any trouble at all but you can't now. It's the traffic that's spoilt everything.

What's your favourite part of the Forest?

Boldrewood. Yes – it's getting spoilt now because everybody's found out that it's the... it's the prettiest road, because it's more natural, I think. In the autumn it's the trees going up to Boldrewood that are so beautiful. On the bigger roads the trees don't meet over like they do on the smaller roads, but even along that main Southampton road on Saturday, I thought it looked beautiful, yes – it's lovely. Just don't look at and listen to the traffic!

John as a young man.

John, Commoner and horseman

Up a long track alongside a Forest heath is a five-barred gate by a barn and beyond, a bungalow. We talk in a parlour decorated with hunting items, a painting of John as an agister, a mounted horse's hoof. Outside, it is an overcast day in November.

I ploughed my first acre when I was twelve years old with three horses, with a double-furrow plough – not in this area. North of Winchester, then, my father was living. That's the only time.... I've been living in the Forest now just on fifty years. 1937 when I come here to live.

Ploughing with a horse looks extremely difficult....

The horse that follows the furrow does the work, really, for you. If he don't stop in that furrow – you know you got your furrow, turned over – a good horse does that, holds the furrow. A double furrow like I used when I was twelve, there was two levers and you'd pull one back to lift it out of the ground and the horses'd turn round and come back into the furrow. But the single furrow plough you had to lift the handles round, which was too heavy for me at that time. Anyhow, I got used to it. I used to love ploughing with horses.

And you're walking behind all day long?

Oh yes. You wore some holes in your socks then. [He laughs.] You did that.

Working horses – grass cutting early in the twentieth century. (OW)

They used to reckon a man to be able to plough an acre a day. Started seven o'clock in the morning, finish at five at night, with two horses. But you had to keep moving.

I remember the first job my father put me at on the farm. It'd been hooked up by a steam plough, the old fashioned... and it was big lumps, big as that down there, that wood box. He sent me up there – I left school when I was thirteen – I was fourteen within a week. Before I was fourteen he sent me up on the hill there and I had two coats on and then I couldn't keep warm. With a horse and roller. It was terrible trying to break these knobs down because there wasn't machinery about them days like there is today. But where this big thing hooked this clayey ground up it was all knobs. I always remember father saying, 'Well, you left school, you've got to work now.' And that was it. When we came down here, my father took this farm, he said, 'Well, I think you ought to find another job to do,' so he sent me to Ringwood, to a man name of Baker, got a cycle shop. First job I had was to mend punctures. Well, I think I made more punctures than I mended and I had – well, with the traffic going by then (it wasn't so much traffic as it is today I know) but, the traffic going by, I had a terrible headache. I couldn't put up with it. So I stayed there ten days. First week and he said, 'You don't like this job.' I said, 'No, I don't!' He said, 'Well, like to go home?' I said, 'Yes, I can't put up with this.' And that was when I came back home.

I was an Agister in the Forest. If there's an accident on the road, which there still is plenty now, more than there should be, you've got to go out no matter what time of night it is and destroy that animal if he's got a broken leg or laying badly injured in the road. I never used to like shooting very young foals. You grab them and it's like getting hold of a child. They don't make a noise. I never used to like grabbing hold of them. But you did and you got on and done your job. You had to do it. That's what you were there for. Oh, they panic. We use a ring rope, it's got a ring, metal ring, long rope and you lasso them. Surprising, you can do it better at night, more than you think for, because they don't see the rope coming. You have a long stick and just drop it over them. I've had several bad ones. I had five one night, in one accident, one chap. Four I shot for him and found another one next morning, close by. He got stopped from driving. Cattle, that was. That was on the Fordingbridge to Cadnam road. I always remember going to Totton and seeing a pony stood up and there was a door handle of a car, caught it here and ripped it right up.

How do you cope with poor animals suffering like that?

You get hold of it as quick as you can and put it out of its misery. Quick as you can. We were given very good little guns, a humane killer, three-two bullet which is extra-strong and you just.... You know the curl that's there on a horse? Inch above that. Or if you had your doubts just draw a cross there, like that, with your finger....

A cross on his forehead from the ears down towards the eyes....

John as an agister, taken from a painting in John's front room.

Forest ponies.

That's right, and where that cross... you know near enough where to put it. The first pony I ever had, he used to do everything. I used to put the collar and hames on him when I had a dead pony down in the woods for the knackerman. The knackerman used to come with his lorry and he [the pony] used to put him in there, drag that dead pony out. And I could even shoot a foal from him.

Did the pony you were riding get upset by dead ponies?

No, he never did. A lot do – snort and blow. I always take him out when you're looking for a dead one, he could tell you where it was because he starts sniffing and you knew you were getting close. I haven't ridden for this last two months, but I still hope to ride. I haven't bothered. I do miss it, yes.

Simon, Forestry Commission officer

A large room in the Forestry Commission's local headquarters – a very old building which has been converted to largely administrative use. As we talk, there are sounds of busy footsteps above us on the ancient wooden ceiling. Simon, young middle-aged, has a candid, outdoor face.

Can we talk about the forestry, the actual cropping of the trees?

Tree planting only started in earnest in the late 1600s. It was a hunting forest up until those days. There'd been odd attempts to plant trees for some purpose, either because they'd run out of firewood or as shelter and so on, but in the late 1600s that's when tree planting became in earnest for supplying wood for the ships of the King's Navy. In the two world wars there were vast amounts of timber removed from the Forest to help with the war effort. There is a nice little tale that they say, that during the 1939-45 war there was enough timber removed from the Forest to build a bridge nine foot wide, one and a half inches thick, which would stretch from Southampton to New York. Mighty lot of timber. I think a lot of people get the impression that the Forest is a museum. It's not, it's a working forest. It's been worked by man and it's been eaten by beast. There has been traditionally conflict between the guy who's been trying to grow trees and the person who's been trying to run a beast on the Forest to make a living. That is not so much today. I would say we're going through a period of where almost all of those parties I've mentioned know that for the Forest to survive, commoning has to survive. Imagine the Forest

without it being eaten by the beast. It would be grass and vegetation, like a jungle. It would be beyond man's financial resources to cut it all to look the same. [The cattle] are very efficient lawn mowers.

I suppose most of your market is on the softwood side?

Not necessarily, no. There's always been a very good market and it's even more nowadays, for oaks and beech. The hardwood market is always very buoyant. But the bulk, here and in other places in the British Isles, is for conifer. Although the proportion of conifer and broad leaves in the New Forest is 60 per cent in conifer and 40 per cent broad leaves, it's getting round to about 50-50 per cent, and we would like to see it go the other way so that we've got possibly 70 per cent broad leaf and 30 per cent conifer. There are a lot

The Queen's House, Lyndhurst, in the early 1900s. It is now the home of the Forestry Commission. (9C)

The Queen's House in 1998.

of trees on the ancient and ornamental woodlands that we don't use commercially. They were used commercially up until the 1970s. During the 1970s there was some controversy about utilizing these woodlands and people saw that these woodlands might fail if we utilized them commercially. The 'ornamental' part is just the fact that they're very old trees and they look very pleasant. A lot of them are pollards, trees that were beheaded by the keepers during the King's days here when they were hunting, to feed the deer during hard times such as January and February each year. So those trees were beheaded and then sprouted again. Those very large mature trees you see now, it extends their life by beheading them. Whereas normally a beech or an oak at two hundred years they've reached their maximum growth and

they start to die, those that have been pollarded can live for many, many years. There's certainly some of 300 or 350 years old in the Forest. There are some in the British Isles known to be 800 years old: beech, which is almost beyond thought.

In January, February every year, you can imagine there's very little fodder left for [the deer] in the Forest. They're competing with the Commoners' animals, they're competing with everything else, so they used to cut the tops of the trees down and re-pollard some, very similar to what you see in an urban area where they keep cutting plane trees down – you know they sprout again, so it has many heads. Those would have been re-pollarded and the animals, when these branches and boughs fall on the ground, they used to eat all the bark and twigs. As a

Timber hauling, early twentieth century. (9C)

result of that, the keeper or others would have had a resource of very nice dried firewood from the remains.

How would I recognize one of these old pollarded trees?

Very easy. Look at any tree and look at it about... it might be five or ten foot high, above that there would be many branches. The most obvious one in the New Forest is the Knightwood oak, which is an ancient pollard. Through Knightwood and up into Mark Ash, nearly every tree there is a pollard. It was in fact banned by Act of Parliament in 1698, but that has since been rescinded. Because of the act of cutting a tree off in its prime, you don't get straight timber for the ships. The idea is that the most valuable tree to a timber merchant is a long straight tree or a short, fat straight tree, but a pollard has many branches. I think the original rule

Tree felling, early twentieth century. (9C)

Forest trees at the turn of the century. (9C)

Modern tree planting. (FC)

Trimming branches with a chain saw. (FC)

for pollarding was to behead it one and a half times the head [height] of a man. How big a medieval man was I don't know. Probably he was a lot shorter than you or I. The actual practice was to cut the tree off when standing on the back of a horse and cart. It would be very much against the Health and Safety at Work Act! The idea was, it was above the browsing height of a deer. Have a look through any of our woodlands where there's ivy or holly, there's a browsing line.... Ivy on plenty of oak crops, you'll see the deer doesn't just eat it head-high, he stands on his hind legs, feet against the tree, and eats the ivy. And that's about one and a half times the height of a man. So any new shoots wouldn't be eaten off by the deer.

What about National Park status for the New Forest – is that the right way to go?

I haven't seen any National Park that's a success. I would say that the New Forest is far more successful being run by people locally than being run from afar. That's my personal view, not the Forestry Commission's view. And I would say that the longer the New Forest stays in the hands of locals, the better it will be.

Since this conversation, the New Forest has been granted modified National Park status.

So, what goes wrong with National Parks?

There are several things. Planning is one of the major ones. People involved in it who really aren't bothered about the area, they're professional people in their own right but don't have the area to heart. Go into the Verderers' Court,

31

A typical Forest smallholding, Pilley.

hear the people who represent, for instance, the New Forest Association, the Council for the Protection of Rural England – those people care about the Forest. The local people care about the Forest. But once you get into national bodies, I think you're losing the identity. I mean, you could say why is the Forestry Commission running it, but at the moment tell me somebody better and I might agree with you. I'm a professional forester and I'm not bothered who runs it, whether I'm run by the Forestry Commission or if a private owner bought the New Forest I could work the same for them.

People tell me that one of the problems of the Forest is the Commission's practice of using contract labour.

I would back them on that. I think the trend nationally in the Forestry Commission – and most government departments – is to contract work out. The County Council do most of their work by contract now, so do the district councils. Any contractors at work here haven't got that same.... There are the odd ones who are Forest people in the contract force, but there are outsiders who haven't got the love of the Forest and the interests of the Forest at heart. I now know who you've been speaking to! [We laugh.]

Dave, Commoner and individualist

Dave lives in a mobile home up a narrow lane in the far south west of the Forest – a healthy, not to say tough-looking, forty-year-old. He has a thatch of black hair under a flat cap; he does not beat about the bush.

I was born 1947. My grandparents brought me up, up the road here, and I've lived here all my life. I only ever worked for a master three months of my working life and I had the sack from there, which was the best thing that ever happened to me really. I used to work for a chap, used to have all the black cattle on the Forest. Me and him didn't see eye to eye; I had the sack and I've been self-employed ever since.

Why was it the best thing that ever happened?

Well, let's put it this way: you're not forever holding your hand out at the

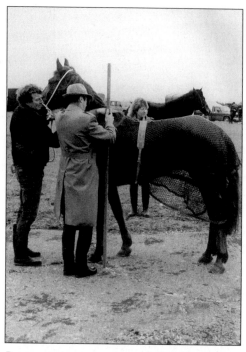

Point-to-point: measuring up before the race. (9C)

A grim day at Hatchet Pond.

'Grockles' (slowly) approaching Lyndhurst, summer 1998.

end of the week. If you don't work, you don't get any money. But there is plenty of work about. All over the place. Don't matter what you do – hedging, fencing, gate posts. I've done painting houses and gardening and furniture carting; you name it, I've sort of done it. I was born and bred and brought up in it. Grandfather used to milk a dairy of cattle up there. Only had ten cows to milk. I stopped there and then I went on my own and done anything; anything and everything. Used to buy eggs and sell them, keep rabbits and kill them and skin them and sell them, when I was sort of sixteen, seventeen. It's been a way of life. It's not what you earn out of it; so long as you got enough

to keep a roof over your head and a shirt to your back and a bellyful of grub....

How do you decide what job you're going to do? How does it work out?

Well, just supposing I'm here today and at the moment I'm putting a new floor in the lorry, right. And tomorrow morning, it'll be about half past five, six o'clock and still dark – get on the horses and exercise them. Back home for daylight, half past seven, eight. So they've had a couple of hours' exercise. Ride them out, down the road here and up in the Forest.

But at this time of year [December] it'll still be dark!

Yes. Well, you can see in the dark! [He laughs.] And then run up to Christmas and then we have our New Forest point-to-point races across the open Forest, which we usually got a horse to run in it. Makes a bit of fun. That's going to start from.... The finish is in the vicinity of the Naked Man, Wilverley, this year. You won't know where the start is until Christmas Day. It's one of the only two original point-to-points left in the country. The other one's in Ireland. And it's from point A to point B, and it's the one who can get from point A, the start, to point B, the finish, the quickest. They don't actually tell you the start, they only tell you the meeting place where you assemble, so you're not taken to the start until the morning of the races. We have nine races – three children's races, a veterans' race and then five other races.

Co-existence: ponies and cars at Hatchet Pond.

What about the hard times?

You do have hard times, yes. Hard times... I suppose it's weather. Autumn can dictate your hard times for next year, because if you get autumn time with rain in the day and early evening, followed by a hard, severe frost during the night and the next morning and then rain again, your mares will abort their foals. Rain is worse than frost. Torrential rain and the odd frost on a Forest pony's back is worse – like we had several years ago, ten, twelve degrees of frost, they can put up with that. They don't mind the dry and they don't mind the cold, but they don't like the cold and wet together. They don't mind the snow. They'll stand up under the holly bushes when it's snowing and when it's stopped they go on out there and paw back the snow and eat. And that to me

is basically your constitution of your Forest pony. If they got the will to live and the courage to get on and do those sorts of things, paw the snow back and eat gorse tops and holly prickles and holly leaves and brambles and things like that, and forage, they're all right. If those Forest ponies broke even every year, you'd be quids in. Or if they made a profit every year you'd be pounds in. They don't make a profit. It's a way of life and without us, the likes of us, there is no Forest.

I'm on the Commoners' Defence Association, which looks after.... We are a body, a committee rather, that looks after the interests of the other Forest people and we do presentments to the Verderers' Court and put in a burning programme, a clearing programme, a draining programme, for the well-being of the Forest. For the grockles [tourists]

35

A controlled burn – an often misunderstood way of conserving the Forest. (FC)

to enjoy. And without us the Forest is lost, those grockles won't enjoy it. Because the Forestry Commission wouldn't be able to manage it without our cattle and ponies there. It would just become a wilderness. A jungle. You see, if so be there was no Commoners' Defence – and it means what it says, Commoners' *Defence* – your defending your rights, your animals' rights.

Against what? Who's threatening?

Who's threatening? The general public. The councils. The Animal Welfare, the Nature Conservancy and people like that, they think that the Commoners are nothing. They think they can manage that Forest without us. We've been trying to get a pond in a place called Akercombe Bottom. It's one of the sources of the Lin Brook at Linford.

It's head of the springs and the water drains out of this valley right up through here, right from as early as June. It dries right out, right the way till September gone, and those animals got to walk two miles for water and that's not their way of life because when it's hot summertime, like we've had a hot summer this year, they likes to be able to shade in the wood, in Pinnick Wood, and walk out to the ditch, have a drink and go back in. Stand up there in the shade out of the flies and the sun, all the heat of the day. They couldn't do that, they had to be on the wander in that heat all the time. We put in for this pond to be done about four years ago and the pond was actually agreed to be done, by us, by the Forestry Commission and the Nature Conservancy Council. They said they were going to start and I was asked by one person, where was the pond going, and I told them. They said, 'Well, you'd better get up there a bit quick because they've been instructed to dig the pond in a different place' – which was 500 yards downstream of where it should be; and where it was in the lay of a hill where the washings off the main A31 dual carriageway was going to come off and run straight in the pond. I went up there and stopped the lot. Then we had another meeting and we had a real set-to row. But we've got the pond and he's full of water, and those ponies are there and the cattle feed there. I haven't known cattle to feed and shade there all my life, but they do now and this year was the proof of it. They needed that fresh supply of fresh, clean spring water to hold them there.

In my own estimation, in *my* estimation – I'm not saying it's wrong and I'm not saying it's right – the Nature Conservancy Council really have got to be educated by the Forest people, not by Forestry Commission, not by their office wallahs – they got to be educated by the Commoners. They don't come and ask you. They just say, 'No – we're going to block that issue.' They just block it.

Sid, New Forest butcher

A neat bungalow in semi-rural suburbia. Southampton Water is not far and the Forest begins just down the road in the other direction. Sid is now retired, a keen golfer.

What was your job, when you left school?

Butchering. I went as an apprentice butcher. I did thirty-some odd years

at that. And there's no money in it and I just packed it up and worked for the contractors where you could earn money. In those days the only regular job you could get was in the food trade. Otherwise it was the building or... like even in the Esso in those days you were in and out of work. You might be working for six or eight months and then you were out for five. There was only one thing to do, go where you were never out of work unless you misbehaved yourself. That's the only reason I went into it. But the money was poor – long hours and poor money. We used to work on average eleven to twelve hours a day, that was at the age of fourteen – you left school at fourteen in those days. Five and a half days [a

Commoners' cattle – a verge-browsing cow.

week]... it was virtually six because when it was your half day you were lucky if you finished by half past two. We had a slaughterhouse in Hythe; we used to slaughter Wednesday afternoons and Thursday afternoons.

We had a humane killer for cows, steers. That was bell-shaped, it had a captive bolt in it. A blank cartridge, captive bolt – used to drive the bolt straight into the head. But before that, before my time, they used to use a poleaxe. I've used one. It's a ... handle about so long... three foot near enough, and you had a sharp edge to one side of it and on the other there was like a whole spud about the same length as my little finger and it was hollow. You used to drive that straight into the head. And then they brought out a new law. If you were a slaughterman you had to register and you had to use a humane killer on all animals. That was like a revolver – it was a two-two but it had a spring-loaded head which you had to push to the animal's head before you could – when you fired. And the first time I did this, five of us in the slaughterhouse and a sheep. Grabbed the sheep and one of the other chaps up and shot it.... We just stood there petrified, because a sheep's head – it's so thin, it's all like layers, the bone and the head. The bullet went straight through it and just went round and round the wall, just waiting and wondering who it was going to hit. Yes, it went straight through the sheep's head – of course, they're so soft – and just ricocheted round and round the wall in the slaughterhouse. I tell you, we never used them again. Not on a sheep. They stun them these days. What they used to do was they just used to stick them the same way as beforehand and then when you dress them you drive a nail through the head so when the inspector came round he thought it was a bullet hole.

You say you stuck them as before. How...?

With your knife, behind the ear. Used to go straight through the back of the ear, then down out that side. Straight through the neck: in one side, out the other. They just bled, that was it. Everything has got to be bled. That's why.... Have you had deer meat? It's always black, isn't it? It's not bled properly. Oh, we've had some fun and games. Same with pigs – you get a biggish one in there, a two-two bullet wouldn't knock them over. It could be quite naughty at times. If it didn't knock them over you used to up-end them and stick them again. Through the throat, that way, and straight down in the heart.

How did the Forest smallholders slaughter their domestic pigs?

You only ever stuck them. My pal and I, we used to go round killing people's pigs for them. People knew that we were doing it so we had the old humane killer and we used to shoot them, but otherwise you turn them up on their back, stick them, and that's it. But the majority of people that had them done, we'd do it down at our slaughterhouse. And of course they hadn't got the facilities for scalding. You could burn them off with straw, but they don't look the same when you burn the hair and that off. When you scald them, there's a thin layer of skin comes off with it.

Commoners' free-ranging stock – pigs feeding on roadside acorns.

Can pigs be dangerous when they get stroppy?

Oh yes. Their bite's worse than a dog, oh yes. My pal and I went to a smallholding to collect half a dozen pigs and they got five loaded up.... The old lady in the house where we got them, she was holding the pigsty door as we were getting the pigs out. Got to the last one, she just got the door pushed up, the last one took a flying leap at the door, knocked the poor old lady over the dung heap which was outside and went haring across their smallholding. It finished up in a chicken coop and my [pal] dived in behind it, pulled the door up and it just crouched in a corner. He went one side and I went the other to grab an ear and as he went down to it so this pig just barked – just as a dog would – and stripped the flesh off those two

fingers as clean as a whistle. Oh yes – they must know.

Do you think they know they're going to be killed?

They get frightened. That is one of the reasons, particularly with a bullock, they got to stand at least twenty-four hours after they been brought down to the slaughterhouse yard. You had a pen for them, because if they're slaughtered when they're hot and after they been humped around in a market and then they get excited, they get what they call 'bone-taint'. The meat becomes rotten within a matter of hours. The meat would go as green as grass.

39

Vera, Commoner and home-builder

A smallholding in one of the Forest's long, strung-out villages. Once the two house dogs are called to heel, I open the farm gate. We talk in the kitchen, where a black log-stove is set in a man-sized fireplace. Vera's husband, Reg, joins us. Also present is a parrot in a pram.

I was born up near the church in a smallholding. Years ago when I was a child everybody had a smallholding. It was all more or less working-class people all down through the village and everybody had a field and they always kept a cow and usually a pig and a few chickens in a pen. This was the way of life because we were more or less as near as we could be self-sufficient. We all had Forest rights and therefore all the cattle and cows used to go out on the Forest in the daytime and only come home at night.

So, could your parents make a living from the smallholding?

No. My father worked at what was then called the AGWI – it's now called the Esso refinery. A lot of it was left to the women to help out, the women and the children. I mean, I could milk long before ever I left school. [Father] used to get up in the mornings at about half past five, quarter to six, and go outside and feed the cows – a couple of cows we had and a few heifers – feed them; and it was always bikes in those days – he used to cycle off over to Fawley to work. He used to get home at night about a quarter to six. Meanwhile, us children – or at least me – my brother wasn't even

Vera's smallholding.

Vera's stove.

interested – used to go and get the cows. Then Dad used to milk at night after he got home. In the evenings, oh, around nine o'clock, we used to go out and rack up – that was give them all a bit more hay round – and then go to bed.

What would your mother be doing all this time?

Mum? Well, in the haymaking times, you know, in the summer, when the hay... that was left more or less to the women and children. They used to get out and turn the grass over to make hay. How it used to be, there used to be one chap with a horse and a grass cutter, George Parker. He used to be the coalman as well. You all did two or three jobs. You used to take turns in having your grass cut. Monk Crouch would have it cut one week, we would

another, uncle Bob another, so on like that, because everybody helped each other. You didn't get paid for it – you just automatically helped. Bear in mind the wives then had a harder life than what they've got now. [Mum] used to go out to work three mornings a week. Used to cycle down to Beaulieu, housework. Everybody did. Down in the Mill House – you know, where the mill is down Beaulieu – in the house next to the mill. And while the men were all gone to do whatever they did in the day, the women and the children used to get out and turn the... the rows, round and round the field... They used to turn the grass to be made into hay. All done by hand. You had a hay rake – a big thing over like that and the tines come down and a horse pulled it. We had a horse called Maggot and we had one called Punch. They used to pull the hay all up

Haymaking, early twentieth century. (OW)

Reg and Punch.

together in... I could tell you windrows but that wouldn't mean a thing to you – a long row across the field. When it was dry we used to turn it up and make it into pooks. A heap of hay, the hay all gathered into a big heap.

People would come in with their horses and carts and usually of a Saturday – nobody worked on Sunday. Funnily enough, years ago they'd let their hay get wet before they'd work on a Sunday. You used to do the *necessary* work, feed the cattle. Mum never allowed me to knit or sew on a Sunday. Used to go to chapel, come home and I suppose have the wireless, and feed the animals. Had best clothes on and went out for a walk Sunday afternoon.

We used to go and get the water in the buckets and we had some little way to carry it up, but it was lovely water, straight from the spring. Beautiful water.

Vera as a young woman.

Vera in 1998.

43

Vera's privy, 1930s.

You know what a well's like, bricked all round on the inside. And then, when you got no electric, everything's got to be done more or less by fire. There's wood to be sawn up, there was wood to be chopped up, because you just heated your kettles all the time. It was an open fire, an open grate and the oven was sitting on the side. You puts a bar across your fire and your saucepans go on there, and the kettles. We didn't have a bathroom though. We used to have a bungalow bath. Before that we had a hip bath. I don't know how many times it got used, mind. The hip bath was up the back, wasn't it! And we never even had a sink. It was a bowl on the table and a tray to turn your cups and saucers up on. I mean occasionally you had smoky tea, but you didn't take any notice of it.

Would you ever go back to those living conditions, if you had the chance?

What, how it used to be, no electric, no water... we couldn't do it now, we couldn't draw the water up out the well, but... as I was brought up I still am now, I see no need to waste. I mean, we got enough money, I'm not going to say we're hard up – we're not, but only for the simple reason we don't want to live high. We got enough for us and if that wood burner's going and keeps us warm it also keeps those kettles hot. And if I want to cook on there, all you got to do is open the bottom up and get it a bit hotter and you can put a saucepan on there.

Are you the last generation who will be prepared to live in this way?

44

Yes, yes, definitely. We have got a granddaughter and we have got a grandson that would love to come here to live. The granddaughter is an absolute natural with the animals. We've got one grandson that likes it, but no way can we let two grandchildren have this place when we have got other children and other grandchildren. I don't blame the youngsters of today. They can go out to work, can't they – work five days a week – and they don't work as we did from the minute you got up till when you went to bed. They can get good wages. The world's got smaller. They go abroad now for holidays. How many holidays have you had, Reg? [Reg laughs.] Never had our honeymoon yet! He's had two holidays since we've been married. There's only one holiday that I've been away with Reg, when our children were small. [To Reg] Then next time you rode your motorbike down to Cath's on your own, didn't you. Not because he couldn't go on holiday....

Reg:
She wouldn't let me go!

Vera:
Reg! He hasn't wanted to.

So what will happen to this place when you die?

This place is going to be sold. It's the only fair way of doing it. It's got to go on the market. It seems a shame, because this will be another smallholding gone and there's not... there's only Millie's all up through [the village]. When I was there all houses had a cow. There's only one person I know up that end of the village that's got a cow and there's about a couple perhaps, down the road. It's progress. We made a living only because we worked hard and we kept the swill pigs. You couldn't do it today. This is what we've said lots of times, you wouldn't be able to do it today.

Freddy, Commoner and village worker

On a frosty morning, we meet outside his cottage. Freddy is standing by a dung-heap, pitchfork in hand. A short, sturdy, thickset man in his seventies, I guess. We enter the house through rows of caged birds, all loudly chattering. We talk across the kitchen table.

He [my father] worked on the Rhinefield beat, Forestry Commission beat. My grandfather didn't; he worked for Rhinefield House. When grandmother done the washing and that, he went round with his handcart collecting the washing from the big houses and brought it home and she'd do it or they'd do it. She got a woman to come from Sway. And then he'd take it back again.

My grandmother used to employ two or three women from Sway – one and sixpence a day, apparently, and bread and cheese dinner. She had a copper, just a copper, with a fire underneath. It was like a brick place in a corner, and then a round copper. Then they used to light the fire underneath, chimney'd go up the side, boil the water then stir it up. They had old mangles... I suppose you seen one – they... squeeze the water

Freddy's cottage in 1998, sold and undergoing renovation.

out after they'd rinsed it and washed it or what the hell they do with it. In those days there used to be a lot of it round... yes, there used to be clothes lines out on the Forest. There used to be Miss Tuck's and Mrs Collins' and there was Mrs Tregunner down Martin's Road, they used to have lines and get out there. A lot of properties – Curtiss's down there – they used to have a line on the Forest, get out there and put washing up.

And they all got washing from the big houses?

Big houses and that.... Big houses here then – gentry, proper gentry, not like they are now – real gentry, real rich people.... Head gardeners and gardeners and chauffeurs and grooms and kept horses... big hunting people, a lot of them. There was plenty of work round here for people then. There's nothing now. The Forestry Commission, they got no men now; they used to have hundreds one time. Now I suppose they ain't got a hundred. They used to have about eight beats; there used to be about a hundred on some of them, working men. You could generally get a job with the Forestry Commission. Their money wasn't very much I'll admit.... Like farm jobs and garden boys and odd men... plenty of men round here.

Was your father able to read and write?

No. If he'd got a paper, he'd only look at the photographs, he wouldn't know who it was or what it was. He could sign his name, just his name, but you had to bide there with him to make sure he done it right. My grandfather couldn't

One of the 'big houses' near Freddy's home. (9C)

do that. He used to put a cross.
Grandmother could write.

Could they reckon money?

Not half!

Geoff, itinerant thatcher

He has a good old Norfolk accent – but has spent much of his life in the New Forest area. A detached brick house on the edge of Southampton. A friendly, hearty man this grey, cold morning, in spite of his painfully gouty foot.

I'm a Norfolk man, yes. We used to travel all over the country for this firm I worked with, called R.W. Farming, North Walsham, in Norfolk. He had fifty-two thatchers, travelling all round the country. It was all gentry's houses and big buildings, you know.

After the war Geoff was invited to work in Hampshire.

They issued me a house up here and arranged for the first job, then all these pubs Strong's had got: the Barleycorn, the Rose and Thistle out at Rockbourne, the Green Dragon at Brook, all over the place they had jobs. I was quite shocked to think all this work was available up here like this and no other thatchers about much. I belted into it, I had to work out in the rain, the snow, I wouldn't stop for nothing. They sent me one or two apprentices. The government used to help me a bit with them, their wages, but I... I rather work on my own really. But I had three or four chaps and we belted away until that bad winter of '63. If you remember, '62/'63 we had a bad old time, long spell. Long old spell, that. And you know, I kept the chaps on and that

Geoff at work as a young man.

the old, good coat on and... you never can wear gloves thatching, you can't. I got up there with a spar hook chopping off squares, but my fingers went so cold... I done the wrong thing. The old van bonnet was still warm from driving there and I put my hands there and... God! Well, I had to put them under a cold tap for a long, long time to get some feeling back. I thought I'd done it. My chaps, they wouldn't get out, they was in the barn. But I wanted to get and show them, you know. Ah, dear!

That business of '63 sort of put the cat amongst the pigeons for a bit. After that I only had one bloke on and probably two sometimes with big jobs, but then I started to get this darned arthritis. I suppose about '73 I started getting this

broke me. I went skint. I used to feel sorry for them because one or two of them had children at home.

What stops a thatcher from working in cold weather?

Well, you see a thatched roof gets wet and then they ice right up. When you get an icy morning – like this morning – if the sun got on it then you'll see the water come off it. It only penetrates a good roof about less than half an inch, but if you get a do like that.... I was on a job up at Sparsholt, there was icicles hanging off that roof three and four foot long and when they start to come off they come down like daggers. I never forget the morning that really did do it.... I had an Austin A40 van, struggled to work and.... woooh, right, go on, get

Geoff at work, some years later.

Geoff in 1998.

gout and arthritis, started getting at my hands and of course that's all hand-work, thatching. But in the meantime, look at the places I did do around the Forest. I should think every village I worked in. I should think so. I had the reed-beds down here for thirty years. All the reed-beds down here at Redbridge. Some hard graft down there. Thatching's a lovely job, mind. Oh, in the summer there can't be nothing better. Up on that roof, you know... you sing to yourself, you talk to yourself. And I've always loved my job. Oh, my word, yes. The people you meet, too: it's not like going to the same factory every day and meeting the same faces. I've met some wonder... look at Lord Louis. Wonderful chats with him. One day he said to me, 'You're a Norfolk man, did you ever work at Sandringham?' I said, 'Oh, yes, sir.' He used to come out on the jobs and have a chat to me when I was doing work on Broadlands Estate which I done for a good many years.

If you had your time over again, would you have done a different job?

Oh, no, I love my job. I wouldn't have worked out in the wet and that quite so much. Probably brought a lot of this on. Driving home, perhaps you'd been working thirty mile away, then driving home in the wet, sodden clothes and that... It got into my bones and got me early in life. They used to say, the old boys I used to work with, 'You'll be sorry, my boy, you'll be sorry.' And I'm damned if they weren't right.

Bob, Commoner and corn-mill worker

A tidy bungalow in an urbanized village, deceptively near the Forest. Bob is a quietly spoken, neat chap. We talk in his bright white kitchen.

Bob with his prize onion, 1998.

My working life started when I was about twelve year old. That was working for my father, jobs around and that. I left school when I was fourteen; then I went into Beaulieu Abbey Mills straight from school. That was on this corn, mostly, from the farms and animal feedstuff. I think I was one of the last ones to use that mill for grinding.

Is the mill still working?

No, I don't think so. I suppose it'd want a lot of repair, more than likely shake the place down now. It was very bad when I was there.

It was a watermill?

Oh, yes. There was two big stones in there and they weighed over a ton each and it was the water that... On that bridge [in Beaulieu village] is some hatchets, some sluice gates, well you operated those sluice gates to operate that mill. When they opened the sluice gate underneath the mill where the wheel was, the water used to come round, down through, hit these big paddles, turn that wheel that drove those turbines. But winter time was a different kettle of fish because if you didn't operate them sluice gates properly in the winter you would finish up with a head of water and that water would build all the way back up to Longdown [some six or seven miles upstream]. You would flood everybody out. We used to grind three or four times a week. And when I said grind, this was not for flour. The flour grinding finished long before I went there. We used to grind the corn for the farmers to feed their livestock. It was noisy and it used to shake, because the place was years and years old. When I first went there, out the back of the place there was a big wooden store and you had to watch where you trod or else you were down through; and if you went down through you'd finish up in the water.

So the store was built over the water?

Yes. It was dangerous, really, when you realize that in one room at the back you could have anywhere between 500 to 1,000 sacks of corn and some of that was $2\frac{1}{4}$ cwt a sack. A lot of weight on there, you see. Yes, and the rats down there... alive with blinking rats. You used to go in there in the morning and... we used to stack corn in lines, one sack down and the other sack was stood on top of it, so when you come to take it out, your top one you could always get on your back and carry it on your back to the winch where you pulled it up to your second floor to load it. But then the bottom one – you had to use sack trucks for that – and you'd see some of this tipped over where the rats had got hold of the corner of the bag, chewed through the bag, thick Westlake sacks; all that corn would dribble out into the water. So you finished up... it's like having two bricks: if you took this bottom one out, that one's got to drop. They used to have the Ministry in there to poison [the rats]. They come in, they put this poison down for three days running. Used to use a lot of Farley's Rusk. The first two feeds were sweetened – although there was all that food in there without putting this Rusk

Entrance to the mill yard, Beaulieu.

The sluice gates near the mill.

51

The millpond.

down, but the old rats liked this Farley's
Rusk. Feed them two days and then put
the same stuff down with the poison in,
which was blue. And when they took
that, they didn't get very far. No. We
picked up ninety-six one time there,
yes. It was nothing to go in the back
there, get a sack – and you always sort
of push your back into the sack and put
your hands up to get hold of it to carry
it – and get hold of a rat. On top of
those sacks. Yes, oh yes! I never seen so
many rats. They were the big, black
ones, these water rats.

*It's a big carry, two and a quarter
hundredweight.*

Oh yes, and I was carrying that when I
was fifteen. And I'm paying for it now I
believe, with back problems. When
you're talking about sacks like that, it

was nothing to have three... because
Middleton's over at Sway, they used to
do hauling for us, and Hollis from
Hythe with their big cattle trucks....
Now they'd bring in might be seventy-
six sacks on a lorry at a time and you
might have three of these lorries lined
up one behind the other, so you had a
lot of stuff to carry! You do that all day
and you get round to five o'clock, you
go to finish work, knock-off time and
you was just shutting up to come home,
then you get John Reed's from
Downton, they would roll up there with
a bloody wagon with about 130 or 140
bales of hay and straw that had to be
carried in through. Because alongside
that mill was a yard and there's an arch,
and they couldn't get under there. It
wasn't until you'd got a lot of this off
and carried it in that they could get
their lorry in that yard. [He laughs.]

I bet you got home, had some tea and went straight to bed!

No. Before I come home from work I'd have to come to Hilltop. We'd have nine pigs in the sty, I'd have to feed them. We'd have heifers that just calved down, I'd have to see to them, get them all milked out, see to the calves. Twice a week I'd have to boil up three coppers of potatoes, mangolds, swedes, whatever there was, boil that up for these pigs so that they have food to go on through... And all this used to happen in one day. In the morning you used to start off and have to go and feed the pigs and do the cattle before I went to work. And some nights I used to get home here might be nine, half past nine, ten o'clock, for my dinner. Oh, yes – and that went on for a very, very long time. So life's not been easy, mind.

As kids, did you play in the Forest?

We had nowhere else to play. Mostly tree climbing, kite flying, hoops – the old wooden hoop with a stick, out on the roads; get trolleys, little trolleys, get them so that somebody pull you on a rope and you steered it with your feet. Birds'-nesting: a beautiful collection of eggs I used to have. But there again, see, you only touched one egg from a nest. You didn't go and pull it all about, no. I expect I had about 200 eggs. We'd be out all day and finish up with one egg – because if you had that sort of egg you didn't want another one. Used to keep them in a big box with cotton wool.

How did you find out which birds' eggs they were? Did you have a bird book?

No, you knew most of the birds. Some birds you didn't know, you could pick them up off those cigarette cards. Local birds, the majority of them, you knew what they were. Two or three of you – always have a spoon with a bent... so that, the little nuthatches and that, you could get in the hole and get their egg out. [He laughs]. Always carry a little tin with some cotton wool in so that you could put them in. Then when you got home you blew them out, blew the yolk out.

Did you catch rabbits?

We lived off rabbits. It was the main food in the Forest. Rabbits, pheasants and pigeons. And deer. [We used to

Bob in the 1940s.

53

Bob (extreme right) at the Beaulieu Road pony sales, 1940s.

catch rabbits] either with wires or with a ferret and nets, or a dog. You had a good dog, he's worth his weight in gold to you. You never see a Forester with a rough dog. He had to be a good house dog and a good dog for to get your dinner. If you were out in the Forest you could always have him with you and if you see a rabbit, well, he'd pick a rabbit up, no problem, if he was a good one. In the Allotments we always put up wires. You used to watch where [the rabbits] come, watch their run. Where they jump – you could see where they landed, where their feet landed each time, so you put your wire in between a jump. You used to make it that big – enough for his head to go through. You had a little stake on him and a thin little stick to hold the wire up. You kept him up about seven or eight inches from the ground, the wire, cock him up in the air. The rabbit jumps and his head goes through and he's there. He can't get out and he'll choke himself. Set them overnight, go round next morning and then see what... go round there and find that... some lovely rabbits and the blinking cats had been there and ate half of them. [He laughs.] They must have kicked up a bit of a noise when they got in that wire and the cats knew what was going on. They get after them. [He laughs.]

How did you catch pheasants?

Catapult, or rabbit wire on a stick. Get a long hazel stick and tie the rabbit wire to the top. When the pheasant went up to roost, he always worked his way over to near enough the trunk of the trees, at night time. They used to go up out in the branches then work their way in. But you used to watch these for weeks and weeks, see where they were. And then you could go along there, you knew they were there and they were settled. You always had a little torch and when you shone the torch up, the old pheasant used to poke his head out to look down the beam of that torch.... You had your long stick there with this wire on and you used to slide him over his neck. And off he'd come!

You cunning old buggers! [We both laugh.]

Yes that's true. Catapults... everybody had a catapult. Always had black elastic – it was like square. You get your own forks. It could take two or three years to get them, because you used to go round the hedgerows, find a nice fork and then you wanted a good shape to him so you had to tie him while he was growing, so when he growed down and he got bigger and bigger, he come the right shape you wanted him. A fork, a V, so you put a bit of string round and you pull it in [so it's not too spread out] – yes, you tie him there and you let him grow for a couple of years. Then, when you wanted him, you went and cut him. He was thicker. You had him up a nice shape then. That was a perfect fork for you. Privet always used to be good; you could get a good hazel; you could get a good gorse one. You always had your black elastic which was done in leather on the ends, leather that went on the pouch and the leather that went round your fork. You never cut your fork at all. Nothing to have your boots with no tongues in – cut the tongue out, because that was nice and soft, for your catapult.

Eddy and Cath, Commoners and farm produce sellers

A moderately large farmhouse. In the farmyard a luton van is parked. Eddy still does a round, taking foodstuffs to local farms. In the lobby is a harmonium and there are deer antlers on the wall. An enormous kitchen, dominated by a great kitchen table. Eddy is an incredible ninety-odd.

I believe your father was a farmer?

Eddy:

A smallholder. We done other things as well, worked in the woods cutting wood, making pea sticks, bean sticks. This is all on the Barker-Mill Estate. We rented the farm. And then we carried on there some years after father died.

The people who live in the Forest now, are they different from the sort of people you knew?

Mostly, yes. There's one or two that you'd call old Foresters on the old Estate. Yet they were all... if they weren't Foresters, they knew the Forest. People know the Forest now, they get their maps out and walk there, but I don't think that's knowing the Forest. How many of them would know how to

New Forest fern gatherers. (9C)

go out and cut bracken? You had a certain area, you see. The 26th of September you had to get your ticket for so many loads. The keepers were most of them pretty good – some of them were a bit awkward. You'd go and get a ticket for, say, three loads of leaves and you never got to the third one. If they asked you how many loads you had – they knew, mostly knew – you'd say, 'Oh, two.' Well, you didn't say how many *more* – you weren't telling lies. You never got beyond two.

How big is a load of leaves?

As many as we could get in the cart. Get up and tread them in – it was quite a performance. When we were out in the woods getting leaves we always used to have our eye open to see if there was any bees around. We'd get out the honey, you see. Of course, you've got no business doing these things. You had to put a sulphur match in the hole [of a tree] to kill the bees. Then you'd cut across – usually with a hammer and chisel after you'd sawed it through – and just knock that piece out and you could get the honey out. This one particular place that we went to out there, we cut in both sides and we thought we was going to take out a small piece and the whole piece came out and left a great big gap half as big as this table. I think we got three bucketfuls of honey out of that hole. Terrific lot of honey in there – great big combs of honey.

We had the gipsies camping just outside our fence. We used to employ them a bit if we had potato digging or anything – we could always get one or two of them to come in.

How did you get on with the gipsies?

Very well. Never ought to have moved them. I've been in their tents. I've tried peg-making but I could never get on

56

with it. We used to have a lot of poultry at that time, running loose. They would go into the Forest and lay their eggs. [The gipsies would] go and pick a few of them up, but then who could blame them for that? We always found, if we wanted any help, go to the gipsies. If we'd lost a cow – mind, we'd give them a little if they found the cow – if we'd lost a cow, either got in a bog or anything, the whole encampment nearly'd go out and look for it. Of course, if you cross them in any way, that was different. They didn't forget things like that. I say it was a mistake even to put them into compounds; that was the beginning of the end of them, the break-up.

Tom, a gipsy

Tom and his wife were living in a council house in a village just outside the Forest boundary, when this conversation was recorded. It was an unseasonably warm, bright winter's day. As we talk in the living room, the front door is open to the sunshine. Later, Tom takes me out onto the front lawn, where he builds a model bender tent from twigs and black plastic sheeting.

I was born at Dibden Purlieu, a little place called Dibden Bottom, in a bender tent. Was gipsies; I am a gipsy. People used to come along there and say, that's dirty old gipsies and things like that; well, we didn't take much notice of them.

A bender tent is some rods bent over and a cloth or something over the top of it. Make it round. More or less like the Saxons used to have, right back in history. We used to use rods – well,

hazel sticks really it was, about an inch thick and about seven to eight foot long. All as we had in there was a box, like an orange crate, to have our food off. No chairs or nothing. All we used to turn up... was a black bucket what [my mother] used to do her washing in, or set [sit] on a box or make yourself up an old bit of a stool. Many a time I've got a bit of straw, a bit of bracken, fern, and made it up in a little heap, put a bit of cloth on it and set on that. The bed was similar – it was bracken, made of bracken, we used to cut it out of the Forest. Mat grass we used to call it. Some of that, and straw, and we used to tuck it back in with a little bit of stick, with a tick over the top of it, and mum used to put coats, anything, down underneath us to keep the water from

A gipsy woman at the turn of the century. (9C)

57

Bender tent. (9C)

coming under. Used to dig a little drain around the tent. That's the bed we used to have because we couldn't get the beds on the ponies and carts, so make it too heavy for the horses to pull and take up too much room.

On the end of the tent, on the front of the tent where we used to go in and out, we used to make some rods up like a teepee and we used to make a fire in the centre of it. Mainly we used to keep the fire going slowly – build it up during the day, get a nice lot of coals inside of it and then he used to keep it nice and warm. Better than any house. We used to live in the winter in the snow and the frost, things like that. We done the cooking on there. We used to stick a big iron bar down in – we called it a kiddle crane – there is one out in my garden now, we used to get it made from the blacksmith. With a hook thing on the top it is, and put the pot on there, or

the kiddle, or get a couple of bricks if we could get hold of them, put them down along the side, put a saucepan on there and make a stew or something.

I went to school. I went sometimes a week at one place, fortnight at the other, sometimes a month. When we used to travel around we used to be close to a school and then we used to go to school. Come in with two or three different families and their children went to school. [The village children] used to get jealous of us and they used to go and tell the School Board – bloke that goes around now if you has a day off, school attendant. They used to find out where we lived and then they used to come up and see my mother and father and we had to go to school. In the summertime we used to go out in the fields, working. We didn't have no school then. We used to bide there for about a week, a fortnight, never had

Gipsy children, around 1900. (9C)

Walter and Mabel.

time to send us to school. We used to do tater picking-up, strawberry picking, hoeing, pulling the doubles with my mother when I was small, very small – just leaving one plant in a place [i.e. thinning a row of plants]. Dad used to go along with the hoe, chop them out and he used to leave one plant – take the weeds out. All sorts of things we used to do – helping my father basket-making, go out with him rag-and-boning, in wintertime that was. Help him make baskets, mats, doormats, saucepan lids, pot lids... oh, my father could put his hand nearly to everything and he taught me my trade, what I knows. Jack of all trades and master of none! [He laughs.]

Walter, Commoner and carter

It is now early spring and Walter's garden already shows colour as I walk up the south-facing path to the cottage. Through the recently added sun-lounge, we go into the living room, where we sit in comfortable chairs – Walter, his wife, Mabel, and me.

I believe one of your jobs used to be emptying sewage pits?

Oh yes, cesspits and all that. I used to take that out on the farmer's field, tip that out. Sometimes they'd dig a hole and tip it in and bury it. Wasn't allowed to start before ten o'clock [p.m.] and perhaps you'd finish up about three o'clock, four o'clock in the morning. It was a stinking job, really. I had one big house down near opposite the pier and Royden House, and there was one or two places up at Sandy Down.

These were the big houses?

Mabel:
That's right, yes. Most of the cottages had the bucket arrangement – toilet in the bottom of the garden and a bucket. But the bigger houses, well....

Walter:
The cesspit was out in the grounds or in the garden. Had to take the manhole cover off and dip it out with a bucket and a rope and put it in some tubs we had in the cart, and then take it out and dump it. My brother, he couldn't stomach it, he wouldn't go. I used to go. Thirty shillings, your night's work.

Mabel:
A week's wages then, you see.

Who employed you, the Council?

Walter:
The people who were living in the houses. You'd do one tonight and perhaps another week or so someone else'd want one done. Generally used to take it out on the farmers' fields, scatter it out on the fields. If we couldn't get it out anywhere, we'd dig a big hole and tip it in there and put the dirt back in on it.

And would you still have to go to work the following day?

That's right.

Mabel:
It didn't happen every night. About once a year, you'd have to do each one about once a year.

And how many trips would it take to empty a pit?

Walter:
Two or three trips, probably. All depends how full it was. If it wasn't

Walter on his tractor.

The Victorian interior of a New Forest 'big house'. (9C)

quite full you might finish about three o'clock... some nights nearly five o'clock perhaps. You was glad for the money because there wasn't the money about.

Mabel, a country girl 'in service'

As above, three weeks later. A bright spring morning in the New Forest.

Well, the thing was, for the country girls living round here there was nothing else, only service. And there were so many big houses all around. I lived at East Boldre so most of our work was on the Beaulieu Estate and that was all big houses. Everybody wanted staff and some people used to keep several, a chauffeur and a gardener or two

gardeners and then you'd have a cook and a kitchen maid and a housemaid or two housemaids according to how big the house was, and a parlourmaid and a butler. The first job I had I was just a general maid. The lady had a companion and she used to do the cooking and I did the rest of the work – I had to work very hard. I had to get up at seven o'clock in the morning to take tea. And you didn't have an electric kettle, you had to light a range and get the fire going and get the kettle boiled to make sure you took the tea by seven o'clock. Then you had a grate to polish, black-leaded grate to do.

Everybody lived in. You didn't get much time off, either; used to get every other Sunday afternoon from about two till half past nine or ten, and one half-day in the week – it was usually a Wednesday, say half past two up till ten. On the following Sunday you didn't go out at all because the other staff had that Sunday off. They always had somebody there. I can remember as a young girl about seventeen – this was a farmhouse, there was moneyed people that lived there and the son had been to farming college and the father'd bought the farm or rented the farm for him to experiment with farming, but they had plenty of money and they kept a staff. I can remember at seventeen working there on a Saturday evening, wearing a uniform which you had to, like a nippy girl in the afternoon – black dress, black stockings, black shoes, bit of white fancy apron and a nippy cap – and you could not go anywhere away from the house where you couldn't hear the bell. They'd ring the bell if they wanted you to pick the paper up off the floor.

They didn't do anything for themselves, then?

Not very much, no. I can remember one Saturday evening going out by the back door and I could hear the fair down Beaulieu, which was an annual thing.... Oh, wouldn't I like to go! You know – but you couldn't.

How did they treat you?

Some better than others. Some were very good. The first job I had was very hard. I don't know why I stuck it as long as I did. I was there about eighteen months. But I had a Victorian mother and she used to say, if I complained, 'Oh, well, that's a good training for you.' And you had to put up with it. Today,

they'd tell them what to do! [She laughs.] Every day there was a different job to do, a different room to turn out. We had a polished hall and the stairs went up like this; and under the stairs there was her riding boots and golf clubs and all sorts of things. I remember, one particular day, taking this all out and polishing under there and putting it back. This housekeeper came through and she said to me, 'Have you had that all out?' I said, 'Yes.' 'Well, I didn't come through when you had it all out. I think you'd better take it out again.' She made me take it all out again. And I had to – there you are. That was how the situation was. There wasn't much you could do about it.

Nip and his friends

A misty day in March. A keeper's cottage: in front a pony grazes on the village green. All around are the silent woods. In a small living room, the air is thick with tobacco smoke. The friends come and go, but at any one time there are at least three, sometimes five or six, sharing the space with me; also a smallish dog and Nip's pipe. All those present are contemporaries, in their seventies, and have known each other all their lives.

Sam:

I started gravel pecking with a peck and shovel up on Piper's Wait here. There's quite a big hole there now. It's still there but they've sort of sloped it off a bit for safety. The keeper was in charge of it and he came and measured your heap and sent the money in and the forester would pay you. We used to put it in a heap, supposed to be a yard

Nip (extreme right) in his local.

high – well, ten yards square was a hundred [cubic] yards.

Was that seasonal work?

No, anywhen it'd come in, because different builders [would] want twenty yards of white, what they called concrete gravel. You'd peck the top off then for that – take the turf off (it was all heather on the top) – and then you'd take off about a foot to eighteen inches of white gravel and put that in a heap. They use that for concrete gravel.

Was it hard work?

Yes, not half. [He laughs.] I think that was as hard or harder than timber cutting... and when you was timber cutting those days you had to swing the axe and then cut the tree down with the

cross-cut. That was hard work, but when you had the old peckaxe about this long when he come out from the blacksmith's – two foot, two foot six. You'd take it to the blacksmith's and he'd line it, he'd make it longer, because you wear it back. It didn't take long to wear it back, pecking gravel all day. About a fortnight to three weeks. And then you had them pointed every so often. Then after you've used them for a week you'd take them down again and he'd point them again because they wear back blunt, see. You'd do that about three times and then you'd have them lined. Say you took it down there it was eighteen inches long, you'd come out with it two foot six long.

We used to start about eight o'clock and finish at four. They'd always allow you to finish a little bit earlier in the gravel

Nip when younger. (PM)

Tree-felling, old style. (9C)

Axemen at work, early twentieth century. (9C)

pit. One of you'd be pecking it out and shovelling it to the other one, see.... He had to catch it in a screen – you know the garden sieves – catch it in that and shake it to get as much clay out as you could. Then throw the other in a the barrow and wheel it onto the heap. Half of it was sieving, look. One'd peck and shovel and the other one'd sieve and wheel. All hand. It was hard work, I tell you. Yes: I had about two years on the gravel, then I went on the piling and pit-prop cutting and timber. Then you'd come into [tree] planting. I helped plant this just behind here [a beech wood of tall trees beyond his garden fence]. That was in 1937/38; they plant through the winter.

Hang on.... Working with the timber – no chainsaws in those days, so it must have been axes and....

...Cross-cut saws, yes. One of you'd chop the sink out – that was where he had to go, you chop a piece out in front where the tree was going to fall, the other one'd chop round it. Then you saw it down. And sometimes you had to get it to go through the eye of a needle nearly, because it had to go straight. Had to go straight or else it'd lodge up in a couple more and then you had some work!

And you'd be using – what sort of axe?

About two foot, two foot three... you don't have an axe handle too long. As you buy these machine-made ones now, you nearly always cut a bit off them. They get in the way if they're too long.

And the head would be how heavy?

66

Trimming branches. (9C)

About five and a half pound. I can remember when I started, I said that I'll get a seven pounder and they said, 'You must be mad.' I asked someone else and someone else and they said, no, five and a half pound. And that was the weight they used, then.

So anything bigger would have been….

Too heavy, that's right. And if you have it too small you haven't got the power.

Does it depend on the height of the man?

Not really, no. You get a lot of smaller chaps that's a bit stronger, stronger than the bigger one, aren't they? You've chopped the sink out, where the tree was going to follow that down, then you chop round. If there was legs

Tree-felling with a chain saw. (9C)

A family group. Nip's father is the young man on the right of the back row. (PM)

on it or roots standing out you chop them off – they're mostly called claws....

Roots sticking up out of the ground?

That's it. It's done to balance the tree as much as anything, I suppose, to keep the tree in its place. You chop that off – always go round backwards. And you'd chop it round as level as the top of that table. And then you saw it down. The lower you got to the ground the better cutter you were. There's more skill to it with an axe than there is now with the power saw because with the power saw you can saw it so much quicker. With the cross-cut, if it wasn't going right you couldn't saw that side a bit quicker.

Nip:
Whereas years ago it took you about, say, three hours to cut a tree – two blokes – takes you about twenty minutes now. You get a big saw and a chap that can use 'un, with a long blade – it don't take long.

And half the effort.

Sam:
Oh lumme, yes. The only thing that's wrong with these things now is the vibration and the noise. Me and his father, we went down near Bramshaw church up in the wood there one Saturday morning. We had to cut two trees down and we was all morning up to one o'clock cutting two trees down. I think it was better to work with an axe

and the saw, but it was harder and slower. No good today because you wouldn't earn the money.

Nip:
You couldn't hear one another talk, could you. I finished up with a chain saw. If you didn't wear ear muffs it don't half affect your ears. And your vibration – I got bad knuckles now, see. I swear that's all it is – holding the saw. But they're quieter now than what they used to be.

When you're cutting into a tree with an axe, can you feel what sort of wood it is?

Not really, no. Some of the trees are a lot softer than the others. You'll get some oak cut mellow – cut softer. Some of them are as tough as old boots. The beech are the worst. The beech are as hard as iron. But the oak, that chops lovely when you get a nice one, beautiful. Leaves the grain there when your axe goes in, leaves the grain down so nice. Looks lovely. Better to work with than chestnut. I think so, yes. Oak I think is *the* wood.

Bill, Edwardian working man

Bill was born before the turn of the century. He lives in a little house made of galvanized iron. On a sharp March morning, the coal fire is roasting hot. Bill, a slim old man with a broad, black leather belt round his trousers, is obviously pleased that someone has dropped in for a chat about the past.

How many were in your family?

There was Fred, me, Gilbert, Neville and Mary. That's all... alive. We had

Bill's house.

69

Forest husbandry, late nineteenth century. (9C)

one little girl, she was.... I was down, we went down the common; Mary took little Lily down the common along with her, down to get the cows. I had a heifer down there, she was expecting to calve anywhen, so I went off down the field, what we called the Clover Piece. The cows and calves was down there, and Mary stop up again' where the wall was. I just filled the tub up for the horses and that at night time. Mary was out picking some wild strawberries, plenty of wild strawberries along there, along this bank, and Lil was playing about with the bloody water. She had slippery boots on – shoes for a girl about four year old. She was either three or four year old then. Mary hollered. I was down there getting the old cow – soon as I opened

the gate the old cow come on up. She knew she was going home to have a bit of cake, linseed cake. I was looking at this heifer and I thought to myself, ah, she won't be long before she has a calf. I run on up there across where Mary was, where she was hollering because poor little Lil, she'd have got her head all wet and part of her shoulders where she slipped because she slipped out with her hands up. I picked her up, Mary took off her apron and I had little Lil's apron, rubbed her as dry as I could. I picked Lil up – she wasn't so very heavy, four year old – I run all the way up the bloody common wi' her in my arms (different road than 'tis now, bloody rough track in they days where all the carts used to go down there).... I gets up the road

70

Forest husbandry, late twentieth century.

there, Mrs Stainer come out. 'What's on, Bill?' I says, 'Lily been and fall in the tub down the bottom.' I kept running, I kept her in my arms and get up the bloody road and mother said, 'What's on?' I said, 'Poor little Lil,' I said, 'fell in the tub down there.' She had plain-bottomed shoes on, look. Only little tiny shoes. Mother got her there – she always kept a good fire – so... kept her in the chair then, she never went outside the door, because she used to get out in the yard, look, along with we. Mary, she went on back indoors and set down with poor little Lil. About a week or fortnight she was bad, we sent for the doctor. He come, he said, 'Do you know what she got? Double pneumonia.' I told mother.

So that was it. She lived about two days and she was gone. She was buried down Bramshaw church. All the schoolkids, old Mr Newey (Mrs Newey couldn't go because she was too fat, too heavy to go down there) – old Mr Newey, he took all the schoolkids down to the churchyard, down Bramshaw. Besides our lot – got Lily and all they to come – another Lily – got they to come. That was it. I said, 'No more.' I wouldn't let no little kids come down the common no more.

Clem, retired forester

One of a pair of cottages at the end of a lane into the woods. We sit in the small living room. Clem's small dog, looking comic and pathetic in a huge funnel-shaped collar, whimpers from time to time, recovering from a recent operation. Clem is gruff, but kindly.

71

I used to have to cycle – all along gravel roads it was then – from Beaulieu up to the top of Stony Cross, and get there for half past seven. If you didn't, you had district officers hiding in the bushes to see if you was... You did. They used to hide along the side of the road waiting to see if they could catch somebody coming in late. It was hard – but forestry was done properly.

It was about 1969 when they split all the beats. In the first place it used to be small beats, but there was about forty men on each beat. Well, then they brought this chap, this Chief Forester from up the east of the country, and they decided to run a production and beats all working in together. [Before the amalgamation] you had so many chaps that done the cutting, you had so many chaps that done the draining and then you had a few which were day work, which done any clearing up, burning rubbish, anything like that.

We used to plant [trees] very close together, five foot apart and five foot between the lines. Then they used to take out rails, stakes, and they used to sell them on the beats. People used to come along, want twenty, fifteen, a dozen. Everything made money, even to flower sticks and bean rods. Different people come in, they could go along to each beat, you see, and you had a heap of rails outside, you had a heap of stakes. If they wanted six to put a chicken run up they could come and buy six stakes. He could come and get three or four bundles of bean rods. Every beat – and there was about six or seven beats – they used to have their own Christmas trees.

When this new business come they wouldn't sell a *dozen* rails, you had to buy *a hundred* or more, so there wasn't any done. All that trade was done away with. That's how all the blokes spoke, about twenty years ago, they said forestry's had it. There was a lot left and went into the oil refineries. Charlie D..., he left and went to Fawley. We was cutting on an open forest and he said the blasted work was so hard and they wanted so much done for so little money that he told them to stuff the job and walked out. He said, 'I'm off.' He went and got a job over at Fawley. The difference was, he went and bought his house not long afterwards – and car and all the lot. Different wages, you know. They paid a tremendous amount more.

I believe you lived in a hut just after the war.

Yes, up towards Beaulieu.... That was an aerodrome and they let the people... as they got rid of the Air Force kiddies they let people go along there and stay in the huts. When I first went there I got a bus to go up there, went round and canvassed for to get a bus so that the people could get their shopping. The huts were all falling to bits.... That's what we got, come back out of the Forces, to live in. They were 14s a week rent; that was in 1948. The council took them over, these huts, so you were paying the council. I was there about nine months, waiting for to try and get a council house.

I was young and... I come back from abroad, and after being out there for eighteen months in the war and then coming home and seeing the daughter for the first time... She was a twelvemonth old, the wife was pregnant when I went out, and then to come

PLAYING FIELD.

OLD 'WAAF' SITE. WHICH AFTER 1947 WAS USE BY MOST OF THE 'AIRCREW' AS THEIR SITE.

The hut site, Beaulieu airfield. (AB)

home and then to go up into those huts was like living in paradise, although they was nothing, they had nothing in them. I went up there on a Saturday with a lorry, it was pelting down with rain.... They gave me the key on the Friday and when I moved up there the ponies was in the hut. A great, big Nissen hut, tin, and concrete floor and there was ponies in there. The door was wide open and the windows was out – we had to put up sack bags at the windows to keep the cold out, until they come along and put some in. They had to sweep all the manure out, which was about two or three barrow-load, and then scrub the floor before we could put anything on there. And all we had was a double bed and two or three chairs, because I was waiting for my furniture to come. We had our sheets and stuff and all you had was one kitchen range in the middle of this room, this great big hut. We started to cook the dinner up

there on the Saturday and we finished up eating a little bit at half past ten that night. That was as long as it took to cook on this kitchen range. In the end we had to pick up all fir cones by the hundredweight, pick up bathfuls, and that was the only thing you could heat the water up to get a drop of hot water to make a cup of tea. It was the roughest times, really, although it was what you made of them – but it was happy to be together.

Who were the other people living in the huts?

Oh, there was all sorts. There were blessed people running round breaking into places, you had to live all in amongst all of them. There was one or two good people, but.... I went into a hut one day and a chap was in there with a carving knife; he was going to kill his wife, she was pregnant. He was

Forest workers, c. 1890. (OW)

throwing chairs against the side of the tin – it was a calamity. I walked in there and opened the door and stopped him. Then the police came and took him away. There was old people up there and all. There was one couple, they were getting on, they must have been sixty-odd, about two huts away from us and they had a deaf and dumb chap there, and blind. The poor devils used to be sitting up there and froze to death in the winter, in January. Cold! And the old chap, he said, 'I've found a way to try and keep my feet warm,' – and he used to put his feet in the oven. Open the oven of the kitchen range and put his feet in there. That's how hot that kitchen range got! You could put your feet in.

Of course the Air Force was in some of the huts still and people was going across and pinching coal out of their bunkers, trying to keep warm. There was lino in all these empty huts up there and a lot of people they was collaring this lino and... creeping over there in the night and taking some of this lino up and putting it down on the floor to stop the cold. You could not blame. The police come up there confiscating this lino, making people take it up off their floors and fining them for taking it. And then they brought all that lino, put it up in a heap and set fire to it.

Gerald, primary school headmaster

A mild April afternoon at a nineteenth-century village school on a crossroads, far from the nearest village centre. All the children have gone home. Gerald and I sit, knees almost touching, in the only non-classroom, the tiny office-cum-staff room.

74

CHAPTER 2
The Social Scene

Entry gates and lodge, Pylewell House.

Gerald's school.

A young-looking, enthusiastic headmaster who began his teaching career in the city, at Southampton.

You've got quite a wide social mix in this school, though not at all the mixture you had in Southampton.

We cater for children out as far as Portmore, Norley Wood, East End and East Boldre. Now in 1985 the village school in East Boldre closed because basically the area didn't bring forth enough children to keep both East Boldre and South Baddesley schools going. I gather it was a toss-up between the two and the East Boldre school closed and the children were transferred to South Baddesley. At that point some of the children decided to – or their parents decided – that they would go to Beaulieu, which geographically is

slightly nearer, but the school bus was laid on to bring children to South Baddesley. I think at that point the social mix of the school changed quite dramatically because up to then the Norley Wood area was probably an area where – or had become an area where – most of the accommodation was owner-occupier. I think the property prices had got to a point where it needed to be somebody who had quite an affluent background to be able to afford to buy. So that reflected on the sort of children that were coming to South Baddesley School. When we were joined by the East Boldre children we gained children who were from a similar background, but equally there is a council estate there and there were quite a few children who probably were the very traditional Forest families. I even the other week heard the story that there

76

was a gipsy encampment out there, so Romany families were living out there. And I gather that some of those families – or the future generations of those families – actually moved into some of the council accommodation out at East Boldre. So it's created within the school quite a cosmopolitan mix. On the whole, they gel very well.

A year or so ago, Lord Teynham's daughter, who lived in Pylewell House – she actually struck up a friendship with a little girl who lived in a council house, one of the few council houses we have got in Norley Wood, and the contrast of Lord Teynham's daughter going to this little girl's house for tea and *vice versa* must have been quite dramatic. Where else could that sort of thing happen? What's happened now, unfortunately, is that Lord Teynham's daughter has become seven and so she's moved on to private school.

How did the East Boldre people take it, when their school was closed down?

Devastated. They were devastated. They raised petitions, lobbied and did everything humanly possible. I came here three years after it was closed and some of the initial comments that people made to me.... 'Of course, they closed our school.' So even three years it was a wound that was still open. We are conscious of the fact that we tread a very dangerous line. Village schools aren't going to be as favourably looked on, as far as the government is concerned, because we are running our own budgets now. We're funded on our own budgets and we're funded heavily on the number of pupils, and so from the viability point of view the village

school is probably under greater threat... and so that is why we work co-operatively now as a group of four schools. It's a bit like the corner shop against the supermarket. We band together and become like the Spar grocers. The school is getting closer and closer to being run like a business.

Ralph Montagu, of the Motor Museum

Quite a small office/study in Palace House, Beaulieu. There are many books, including the ten-volume edition of the Oxford English Dictionary in black leather, which I envy. We sit opposite each other, at a desk. He is pale, fair, with fair eyelashes. He has no upper-class accent; he is friendly and fluent. In 1985 Ralph Montagu inherited a large part of the Montagu Estate, including most of Beaulieu village.

I didn't realize that there were still villages that were owned by a single individual, or an Estate.

Well, I do not own everything, but I am the principal landowner and I certainly own just about all the land that is required for the changes we want to make. I think one point I ought to mention is of course the reason that the plans have been scrutinized in such detail from a design point of view by the planners: it's that Beaulieu is in the New Forest, it is very attractive, it's a Conservation Area and it's also classified as an Area of Outstanding Natural Beauty, so there couldn't have been a more difficult set of requirements to satisfy. I would like to think that

The gateway to Palace House, Beaulieu.

even without those restrictions we, the Estate, would only carry out work which improved the environment of Beaulieu village.

I always felt that since Beaulieu already has a mixture of housing types, there was no reason why, if it was appropriately designed, there should not be a twentieth-century element, just as there's a nineteenth-, eighteenth- and seventeenth-century element. The planners take the view that what we build now should be in some way a copy of that which is around it and should be as low-key as possible, verging on being apologetic. Of course, if we get it wrong, then the more low-key it is, the better. They are right to be concerned, but I wish they could take a slightly more positive approach. I'm afraid this country has gone from being totally insensitive in terms of planning to being almost over-sensitive.

How have you managed to avoid the mistakes made in Burley, for instance, of rows of gaudy tourist shops monopolizing the High Street?

Yes, well, I think we have, to a point. I agree it would be awful if Beaulieu was like Burley, but when I used to walk up to the village with my nanny as a child in the 1960s, every shop provided a service to the village. Now, most shops are primarily concerned with selling to visitors. Fortunately what they sell is of a different quality to Burley, and because there are still people living in Beaulieu there is still an element of providing a service. The Abbey Stores is still a grocery shop, there is still a working newsagent and the old

78

Kitsch – a Burley village shop window.

Beaulieu village, with the old mill entrance.

Cadland House, former home of the Drummonds. It was demolished to make way for the oil refinery at Fawley. (9C)

hardware shop, although their merchandise is primarily aimed at visitors, still has useful things in it as well. There is still a working community around us.

You must be the main employer in the area.

Yes, but most of the people we employ are working in leisure and tourism, in some aspect of the visitor business. Those [he points to a wall chart] are the Estate staff, fifteen of them or something, whereas in total we employ about two hundred.

That's an enormous switch from forty years ago.

Yes, and in those days we had a huge Estate maintenance department, we employed a lot more people in the

woods and of course a lot more people were employed by tenant farmers on the land.

The Forest is ringed round by Estates such as yours. Do you large landowners ever confer together about the New Forest and its environmental problems?

Not in quite the way you've described but, for example, all the owners of coastline along this part of the Solent, which are Exbury, Beaulieu, Cadland, Lepe and Pylewell... Sowley – Sowley hardly own any coastline because they've sold it all off – there is the North Solent Protection Society, we're very involved with that. I wouldn't say we talk to each other much as employers, because most of them are not big employers any more. Maldwyn Drummond [at Cadland] is related to me anyway; he is my mother's uncle so he is family, and I find myself seeing quite a lot of him. My father has always been keen to retain good relationships with all the neighbouring landowners, but I wouldn't say there was any official forum which brings us together.

I just wondered whether the other landowning families had as much concern for the Forest environment as you obviously do.

Well, I'm not sure, to be honest. I know Maldwyn Drummond definitely does. He and I think along fairly similar lines. The other landowners I don't know well enough to know whether they are simply managing their Estate in the way they are because there's no alternative, or because they want to do it that way. Certainly I have found myself questioning some actions taken by neighbouring landowners in the past.

Luke, gamekeeper

Behind the unassuming house is a stunning garden – a long strip running down a slope. Luke shows me apple trees he's grown, bird boxes for tits and flycatchers; there are three blackbird nests in a row under the eaves of a shed, from one of which the yellow bill of the sitting bird protrudes. Luke is in his eighties, tall, long of head. Indoors, we talk in a room with photographs of deer and of gamekeepers on the walls.

Forest cottages, Type 1. (9C)

Forest cottages, Type 2.

I was born at Holly Hatch, in a New Forest cottage. Our nearest neighbours was half a mile away and that was up the farm. The nearest village was three miles away, which was Fritham. Nearest town was Ringwood, that was nine mile. If you wanted to get anywhere, you had to walk.

You must have been quite lonely.

It was remote. I've heard my mother say she haven't seen no-one outside the family for six weeks. That's how quiet it was. I went to school at Fritham, which is three miles to the nearest house and a little school half a mile on; it was three and a half miles each way to walk. And you had no hard surface road, only forest tracks to walk up. And don't forget, in those days there was no such thing as rubber boots – you had only ordinary boots to put on and there's a lot of water gets through them. You get heavy weather, the river'll flood out over and you couldn't get over the foot-plank. Father come down there afore now and waded through the deep river to carry us over. That happened a good many times.

Luke speaks now of his adult years as a gamekeeper.

Egg collectors. Shrikes, different types of shrike. You only find them in certain places and you know where to look for them. Egg collectors again – I've prosecuted one or two of them. I remember the last one I caught, I see him take some red-backed shrike's eggs, I was keeping watch on him. Took these eggs and I was waiting for him to come back up round where he'd parked his bike. When he come out round there I walked out – I walked out too soon. He tipped them on the floor and... [he makes a squashing sound] – so my evidence was gone.

You must have had to deal with deer poachers too. They operate mainly at night, don't they?

Yes. I remember one occurrence... a place in the Forest called Frying Pans Bottom and I was going down along from Boldrewood down into Emery Down one day and I had an under-keeper with me. I looked... I said, 'Dead deer down there.' He said, 'Where, governor? I can't see one.' I said, 'No, but you see a blob of white? Well, that's a deer's belly. She's laying down and blowed' – when they die, they blow themselves up – 'down in the bog right down there.' So he went off down there and there was a dead doe. And a little fawn laying beside his mum, still alive, and he had a ring made all round his mum where he was trying to suckle her. And don't think that didn't hurt this [he points to his heart]. If I got hold of that bloke I'd have done him some damage too – to shoot that doe. He didn't get her because she ran off out the car lights, down on the valley, and left that little fawn alive beside his dead mum. Course he'd gone too far, you couldn't save him, so we had to put him down. Two gone: that's poachers.

Some of these carcasses, they get near £100 for them. Get two or three deer of a night time and they're well away. They come up in the headlights of a car, or else they had spotlights, turn a light on to them and another one'd shoot them. I've had some lovely deer killed.

A New Forest keeper. (9C and H)

Some of my real friends. I had another one, he had five brow tines, used to hang right down low, and I named him Droopy; and he knew his name.... 'Come on, Droopy,' and he'd come on to you, take stuff out your hand. I went down one morning, I couldn't see Droopy. I couldn't understand it because he was always down there waiting for me. I walked out round, come across Droopy out in the heather and gorse there, dead. So I took him in, opened him up. I found a cross-bolt – shot this cross-bolt in there and that had gone up through his innards and right up into his liver. He'd run off away and died. He was one of my pals, he was. I think I'd have done that feller in, put a cross-bolt through him if I'd got hold of him.

The estate of affordable housing, Brockenhurst.

Thing I'd like to see stopped is buck-hunting in the Forest. Fox-hunting is bad enough, but buck-hunting – I've seen terrible things with deer. Record that, and I'd say it in front of anyone, I'd like to see deer-hunting stopped. Terrible things. I've seen hounds catch a deer and nobody with them, they'll pull a deer to pieces. You hear the poor deer crying, hounds killing him, pulling him to pieces, no-one with it. I've had to deal with this type of thing; what I've seen, I believe.

Did that happen very often?

Quite a few times. Quite a number in my time. The hounds caught a deer down at Holly Hatch when we was down there in 1937 – bit later than that probably – caught a buck there in the stream, close to the cottage, pulled him

down. No people with the hounds at all. So I had to go down and drive the hounds off and put the deer down, because he was tore, where the hounds tore him. And if you ever hear a full buck cry – a doe's cry is bad enough – but hear a mature buck crying, it's a noise you'll never forget. And I've heard that a few times. It's pitiful. There's only one way to kill deer and that's to shoot them properly. You've got to cull deer. All done by twelve-bores one time, with proper buck shot – and then the deer shouldn't be shot more than 30 yards to make sure of him.

Ron and Sally, Housing Association tenants

A new semi, built by a Housing Association providing affordable housing for local people. It is in a cul-de-sac where all the houses are built by the Association. The design is impressive, with quality and good taste. It is a May evening; Sally is nursing the baby. Ron and I talk at the other end of the darkening living room. Born in the Forest, he had moved out of Hampshire for a while.

When you came back to Brockenhurst, you got married?

Yes, and looked for somewhere to live. Couldn't find anywhere, not round Brock, not anywhere we could afford, so thought we'd try for the mobile home, caravan sites.... Wrote to the Fleur [The Fleur de Lys, a well-known New Forest pub, with a small caravan site next to it.] and enquired at three, four others. Went and looked at several but some of them were rather big – just too big and estatey-like. One at Dibden was huge, not very private. And a lot of them are only retirement ones and we liked the Fleur... quite nice, and what we could afford – that's what we plumped for. We bought it over four years. And you pay ground rent, £10 a week ground rent. I think that's fairly cheap compared to some of them.

We did think about a Wimpey at Lymington which is for first-time buyers, but then again that was an estate, which we didn't like. Or I suppose we could have got a flat. Restricted, aren't they, flats, and they're not all that easy to come by. One or two people who live here, they used to live up on Setley. There's a big house that's split into quite a lot of flats. That's quite a starters' place for young people. Funnily enough, there used to be one just over the road here. I don't know if you saw those very

new places just over the road here – that used to be a big house, that used to be all flats; they've all gone now. The old house has gone, it was all pulled down. Now it's two or three modern places, all sold off.

There's a few to rent if you don't mind a flat, but there's not much choice. Why shouldn't I, if I wanted to, be able to buy a house in Brockenhurst for a reasonable price? I've lived here a long time, why should I have to be rich and wealthy? It's not fair, is it, really? You either have a flat, or maybe a mobile home, and then it jumps into – round here – very rich before you actually own something. There's not very much in between, like these [Housing Association] houses. I mean, they've done these now, but I don't expect they'll build any more here. It's taken long enough to build these.

How long were you in the caravan?

Six years. We liked it. Especially this time of year. It was nice; we enjoyed that. If we could have picked the caravan up and put it in our own bit of ground somewhere around here, we would have done that.

Ken, Commoner and oil refinery worker

It is now early summer. Ken's house is up a tree-lined track. The pines smell of warm sun. On the tape, birdsong is heard clearly above the conversation. Ken, a small, wiry man, took early retirement from the refinery. His wife, Jill, has the quick

The Fleur.

Caravans at the Fleur.

movements of an active woman. We are joined by their daughter, Helen, a healthy-looking pony-rearer. Ken starts by speaking about his first job.

Threshing, threshing. It was a tractor – he'd just got rid of the steam one and it was a big Case tractor and we used to do all the farms from Lymington right over here to Fawley. In those days there was twice as many farms as there are today because they've amalgamated them all. You had eight real big farms in just this little corner.... And quite a lot of all those people that worked on those farms, that I knew, are still alive.

Are any of them still working on farms?

One. One that's still my age. We went to school together; he's still the main tractor driver on the big farm. Early sixties, that's when the change started. Jock, he lived just up the road from us, he went as caretaker in the school. Eddy went as a postman. Jack, he went into the power station and of course I went into Esso.

Jill:
You all tended to go into industry. It wasn't farming any more, farming was dead.

So you made the right move?

Ken:
I made the right move as far as... financially, lifestyle, yes. But job satisfaction was virtually nil in the refinery. You were just turning out all the different products; you could work in there for a year and probably never see any of the products because they

Ken.

were all inside pipes and tanks. You were operating equipment and it was so cold... being on a car line... and you are solely a number in the oil industry. You all have your own number and that's solely what you are.

When you were talking about the refinery just now, you used the word 'cold'. What did you mean?

There's no personal feeling between management and the men. They're solely supervisors, *they're* on the staff side and *you're* hourly paid. They've only got one thing in mind and that is their own promotion and you are just a number to them. The longest a supervisor will be with you is probably

87

A steam-driven threshing outfit, early twentieth century. (OW)

Ken, a milk delivery man in the 1940s.

Ken on the Case tractor, 1950s.

two years. If he's on your job any more than two years he's not very good. He's a has-been. I'm talking of people that – they've come out of university and gone into the technical side and they stay in the technical side for a year or so and they're put out into the refinery as a supervisor, part of the plant. Those that didn't make it either go back down or back into offices and you're just kicked around for the rest of your time. When you're on the farm you were like a big family. The farmer knew you – it was the personal feeling there all the time. But working in industry it is a cold feeling; when you go there they tell you that they'll pay you good wages but don't expect.... They look after you. Really a great firm to work for – if you must work in that situation. They pay such good wages that a lot of people have gone in there, like I did myself. After a month or so I thought, 'Well,

I'm never going to stick this.' But the wages are so good you find that that overtakes.... You just put everything else... you just put up with it.

Why did you think you weren't going to stick it?

Jill:
Well, being *in*, for a start, for you, wasn't it?

Ken:
Yes, being in one area. When you were on agriculture you didn't feel tied. But in the refinery it felt like a prison. Everybody says – I've had it said to me numerous times already and I've only been retired three months – 'What's it like now you've finished your prison sentence?' That's really what it felt like. I'd go in there at six in the morning; if I wanted to come

89

A refinery tank.

Oil refinery pipelines.

back out I would have to get permission to come out.

What was your job?

Working on tankage. Movement of oil around the refinery. When the tanks was filled, the biggest crime was to have one over the top, as they say – overfill a tank. It's a very dangerous situation, because most of the tank roofs are floating roofs – the roof floats on the oil, goes up and down with the oil, so when one is overfilled, the roof is right out over the top of the tank. We had a certain sort of crude from the Middle East called Amna crude. In the winter it was very thick and to keep it liquefied you had steam on the tanks to keep the tanks warm. The supervisor came round and said we were going to have this thick crude coming in and it had to go into special tanks and also we had to

A pony, with tail protruding, confined for tail marking and branding.

keep it at a certain temperature; we didn't want any problems with it. One of the operators had one over the top – he forgot about it. It went over the side of the tank, down into the bay [inside the retaining wall of the tank] and they had to dig it out. It was in the winter and as soon as it got outside the tank it went solid.

All about drifts

At Beaulieu Road pony sales, with crowds around the pens and round the auctioneer's ring. The people seem to be mostly locals – friends hail each other and snatches of news and gossip are picked up by my tape recorder. I meet Helen (Ken and Jill's daughter, see above) and we get talking about drifts – the pony round-ups which are held in late summer or early autumn each year.

You meet usually at the pound. You meet there about ten – which is a bit flexible. They're a bit flexible on the south side of the Forest. North of the Forest is... a different time system. Your walkers are given instructions where you've got to stand out, to help line up... guide them in the last little bit into the holding pen. Then the riders go off and try to bring them in. They'll go out one, two, three, four, five times, different ways, depending on the area, different directions. They usually finish driving by midday – which is anything between twelve and two, depending on what they've got and how many they find; then they stop for a bite of lunch, usually. Then they start working them through to the actual pound, to tail-mark, worm and everything, which will go on till anything between two and half past four – depends on the numbers and how it all goes. If it goes well it's

91

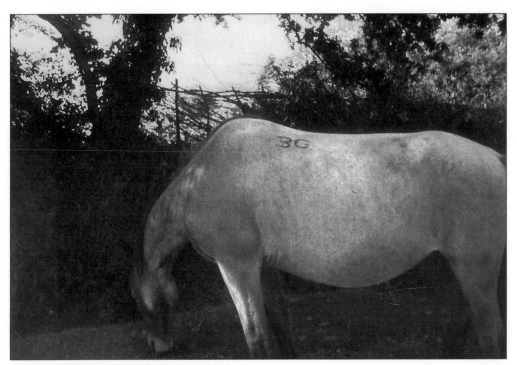

A branded pony.

Ringwood cattle market just before closure, 1990. (SN)

The site of Ringwood market, 1998.

like a piece of cake; they just go out, the ponies come in and no problem. If it goes wrong it's one almighty catastrophe and everybody's blaming everyone else. Hilltop and Ipley are both usually fairly good drifts; the ponies come in well. Withy Beds... that's a pig of a place. We got sixteen on the first day, and that was bleeding good going. Well, it's better than the one they had one year. So sixteen is really hot stuff.

Theo, auctioneer

In his office in a busy market town. There is constant traffic outside the window. Theo sits opposite me across a plain desk; a tall, thin man with dark, wavy hair. He talks almost without a pause. It was his firm that ran and then wound up the only New Forest cattle market, at Ringwood. On the last market day, Theo had been the auctioneer.

Why did you decide to close down Ringwood market?

The District Council had re-allocated the planning use of that area of Ringwood to 'commercial' and therefore for redevelopment it was very much more valuable, so it's the value of the site, really... increased too much to warrant the continuance of a very small, local Forest market. Whereas one's heart was very much for the Forester and the Forest etc., to keep it open if we could, commercially, sadly there was only one decision in it really. From every other point of view it was nice to carry on because it was a great gathering place of the Foresters and the locals and the schoolchildren and the tourists. I'd been there twenty years, I suppose. About 1971 I started, initially not being involved with the cattle side, but then a partner retired and so I moved up into the livestock section and got particularly involved with the Foresters' side of the life.

In the last twenty years it maintained its position very well – we were getting as many calves, store cattle – goats in particular seemed on the increase in the Forest area. But the big changes had really already occurred, that was the trouble. The 1950s was the peak of the Ringwood market when we could have sold 200 fat pigs or store pigs each week, fifty dairy cattle or store cattle, but the change in the way of life in the Forest and the rules and regulations relating to the Ministry of Agriculture – as far as keeping pigs in the Forest and reduction in the small dairies that used to abound in the Forest. Lots of people just having ten or twenty cows which they market through Ringwood because they enjoyed it and it wasn't really worth their while going another twenty or thirty miles to the next one. So those little Forest holdings disappeared in the 1950s through the 1960s and '70s, but reached a level from there on which we maintained. But really there was such a reduction in turnover [from] averaging, say, 200 pigs a week; if we sold ten a week – and not always ten – I mean there's a considerable difference in turnover, and we base our returns on turnover and one's overheads are matched accordingly. But Forest ponies and all that sort of thing, we had a very good little sale of Forest ponies – might have had ten or fifteen or twenty a week of those, which was consistent because they're always there and still there. But

it was the dramatic change, mainly due to Ministry regulations which... had to be, probably, for various good reasons – for the pig side, where for example swill feeding wasn't allowed any more. And then also the dairy regulations as far as not making it economic for the small dairies of ten cows or twenty cows to survive.

Plus, I dare say, the value of property in the New Forest changed dramatically from being an agricultural area to a non-agricultural area.... People live in the Forest with a paddock, for the enjoyment of the environment, and are not dependent on the Forest for their livelihood. So you had outside influences increasing values of property, outsiders therefore coming in and the whole way of life in the New Forest changed. So livestock in general were not the same numbers as they used to be.

The day the market closed – was that just a normal market day for you?

It was not normal because we obviously realized it was a special day, sad for most of us, for some it was probably an emotional day. We made a bit of an occasion of it, whereby we had special stalls, we had music – organ thing – and various events going on to try and record the fact that it was the end of an era. Although our turnover wasn't ever huge, everybody had a special thought for Ringwood and on that particular day supported it, so we had a very large market, for Ringwood. Even if it was that size of market every week of the year I regret it wouldn't have changed the basic economic facts as to its viability, but for a one-off day it was

Riding to hounds. (9C)

absolutely packed with people. Everybody who had memories of Ringwood was there; everybody of course wanted to sell the last animal. Fortunately we got the right person, I think, to do that, and pictures were taken and speeches were made in a quiet, friendly sort of way. The ring wasn't a big ring in the first place and probably defied all Ministry regulations, but there was just room for this little black Dexter cow and her calf which this very old friend of ours from Burley wanted to be the last one. There was just enough room for this animal in the middle of the ring – the rest of the ring was full of people, it was that packed. So, it was nice. I think everyone entered into the spirit of it and values were memorable too because they were prepared to pay that little bit more to just record that they bought one of the last animals sold through Ringwood market.

What's on that site now?

Ringwood is now a supermarket.

Sir Dudley Forwood, former Master of the Buckhounds

Sir Dudley has asked that I use his real name, so I have. His is a medium-sized house at the end of a long farm lane. Sir

Dudley is watering the flower beds, wearing a cardigan and gardening trousers. Inside the house, an indoor pool looks inviting this warm summer morning.

My father went to war, the First World War, on a charger. And, in fact, I've got pictures upstairs of him in France, on the charger. And when that charger was killed, he had one more and when the war was over, in 1919, he brought this charger back to England. I used to ride with him, when he still had his charger, in the New Forest.

I was taught to ride and then my father took me out with himself and my pony to a meet of the hounds. I think you've read in many books the thrill of the horn and the cry of the hounds – soon got into my blood and I loved it. People came to the meets of the hunt in governess carts and ponies and traps from quite as far as eight or nine miles away.

I suppose the hunt was a great social occasion?

Oh, very much so. And, I'm afraid, in those days, a great deal more snobbish than it is now. When I was a boy you hunted with a great deal of privilege. You had people looking after your horse. You could even, in the very early days, have your horse sent on a meet with your groom and perhaps, before cars, you went in a pony and trap to the meet.

And remember, in the larger houses the staff – although people don't like to acknowledge this but it's true – in the nice and proper big houses the staff were in a funny way part of the family. I mean at Burley – she died the other day

– but there was a Rosie Carpenter and she was a kind of second nurse to me when I was a child, and I always retain a great affection for her. And there are people living in Burley now who I remember as 'the grandson of the head keeper at Beaulieu'. The head keeper at Beaulieu was a very important person.

Do you still maintain contact with those former members of your household staff?

Well, I hate to say it, except for one who lives in Switzerland, they're all dead. They were older, you see.

Dan, Commoner and foundryman

A roadside cottage, a small living room, a small Jack Russell dog. Dan has the thickset Forester's build I am beginning to recognize, and the blunt candour. It is a late May morning – the gorse on the heath is blazing yellow. [Tragically, since this conversation was recorded, Dan's house has been destroyed by fire. No-one was injured.]

I've lived in this lane all my life. I've lived in the lane sixty-nine year.

What did your father do?

A smallholder. We used to turn animals to the Forest as well. His father was the same. We've always rented land and I rented from Beaulieu Manor, but when Showerings took over I lost the land.

We walked till you was old enough to ride a bike and make a bike up and then you used to ride to school. Get all the spare parts and then make him up.

Dan and his wife, Rita.

Dan (centre), ferreting, 1950s.

Dan's family on an outing, 1950s.

There was the old dumps in them days that you could find bicycle frames and all the parts in. Not like today – I mean to say, there was no dust carts or anything so everybody got rid of their rubbish in these dumps. Tin cans – well, most tin cans was burnt with the household rubbish and dug back in the garden, but big stuff like old tin baths and bikes and things like that was all put in these old dumps. There was one up in the Forest, there was another one on the corner of Bull Hill. We knowed near enough where all the dumps was. A bike was only £4-odd them days, but who had £4-odd when they was bringing up a family of kids, to keep going buying bikes?

So, making up a bike was something you had to learn to do when you were still quite young?

Yeah, yeah, yeah. And one used to teach the other one. Brothers [taught me] I suppose. Only used to be a three-speed, and a three-speed bike you could near enough do yourself, knock the cogs and that out and put new springs in. Three-speed was a low, a normal and a high and the bigger the driving wheel the less you pedalled. You could buy a big driving wheel with the pedals on or you could buy a small one. A woman's was generally a small one – they pedal a lot faster. But the slower you pedal the harder the work, really.

What did you do after you left school?

I went into Wellworthy's then. [A local factory which made pistons for cars and aircraft.]

What was your job in the foundry at Wellworthy's?

Melting the metal [aluminium] down, at up to 730 degrees, pouring it and making pistons for cars or planes or what. With a ladle, into a big die.

So how many people were there in that one shed, casting pistons?

Fifty to sixty. You was only working in your vest and trousers. Sweat used to run off you. Used to come round with barley water and salt tablets. During the war, night time, everything was shut up, blacked out. You come off nights on the Sunday morning and you'd start days on the Monday morning. Used to do twelve hours, that's what you done, twelve-hour shifts. You had all the smoke and that, because you had to clean your metal off, look. You never just used that as it was melted down. You had a powder to go on and you had a tablet to be pushed down and

Casting aluminium pistons, Wellworthy's. (L)

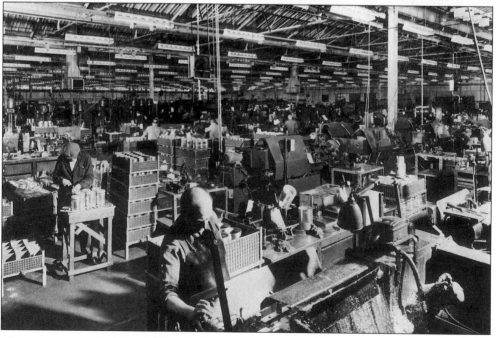

The machine shop, Wellworthy's. (L)

Hand-milking outdoors. (OW)

underneath with a plunger to take the gas out. If any water got in, it'd blow up like a gun. I put a bar in one night, it was getting hot, the metal was going up too high – you had a thermometer in there all the time – and there was a bar on the side of the pot that had been there some time. He was hot, ready to stick in if [the pot of molten metal] got too hot. I put him in and he was dirty and he blowed up like a gun. I had a shirt on but before I could put my shirt out it had burnt through my belt and my bloody trousers fell down. And you was diving about trying to get the bloody stuff off you. I've seen blokes where it'd come out and gone in their boot and couldn't get their bloody boot off and have burnt right into their flesh. I've seen blokes start at seven o'clock in the morning and

before nine they've packed it in, they couldn't cope with it, the heat and the work.

During your time off, were you still looking after your animals?

Yes. See, if you come home from Wellworthy's first thing in the morning and you thought you was going to bed for the day, it wouldn't work because by dinner time you'd had a sleep and you was awake, so therefore you didn't go to bed till after dinner. Have a cup of tea, and might be a bite to eat and then you done what you had to do and then you'd go to bed at dinner time.

Get up for work… when?

100

Wellworthy's in decay, 1998.

About hour before you started. Just have a bite to eat, have a wash and away. Milk the old cow and away.

Dan's wife Rita has entered with tea and biscuits.

Dan:
[To Rita] Or else you'd milk the cow....

Rita:
Well, she was quiet enough. She used to stand out there, you could milk her just out there in the road.

Dan:
Then let her go again and she'd be back here again in the morning.

Did you use all that milk yourself?

Yes – make butter. But it's different today, my sonner! Put it through a strainer, muslin.

Rita:
Then we used to put it into big pans, stand it overnight. Then you had a thing like a flat scoop that you went all round and you took all the cream off and you just left the milk behind. Pigs used to have that. Then we used to make the butter. Did you know you have to wash butter? When you make it you have to wash it to get all the milk out. In water: you move it about with two paddles until you thought all of it was out; and then we had one of those big marble slabs – put the butter on and you beat it all the rest of the way. I used to make all my own jam, bottle all the gooseberries, plums, rhubarb, everything.

Dan:
See, you've only got to go back forty years and you knowed everyone here, but you don't now. There's only about three or four of us in the lane that was

101

Open space in the Forest.

brought up together. [The newcomers] got a different way of life but they don't want to come airing their views with us. As long as they keeps theirself to theirself we'll do likewise. You don't have nothing to do with them. I wouldn't have nothing to do with them. Just pass the time of day and they goes their way, you goes yours. But if it'd been one of your ordinary neighbours you'd stop and have a yarn. Anybody comes here and says they had a problem, could you help them, one of the neighbours, you'd turn round and do it, wouldn't you? But if one of these others come here and said they had a problem I'd say, 'Well, I don't know anything about it.' And they'd have to go away, wouldn't they?

Steve and family, newcomers

They live on the outskirts of the village in a smallish detached house. In the living room the two children are already in pyjamas although it's quite early in the evening. As we talk, dusk falls and Steve's wife June takes the youngsters off to bed. When I leave there is darkness, a full moon, a low mist over the damp patches of Forest road, where the air is suddenly chill.

You've now lived here for five years. How do you think you've fitted in?

Steve:

I think generally we've fitted in quite well, obviously helped by having children at the school because that gives us more direct contact with other parents.

June:
We had a dog when we moved in; as we went out for walks people were stopping and chatting to us.

Steve:
Just after we moved in people stopped at the gate when they went by and sort of said hello and introduced themselves.

June:
Someone said to us, you want to join as many things as you can so you get to know lots of people. I think that's what we did, really.

Steve:
Got involved in the PTA at school; now I'm a parent-governor at the school. One of the things that was very good was that every pancake day they have a pancake party, and the new people coming into the village are invited to that, free. The people that have been in the village, in other words have been through their first free visit, they bring bits to eat along, sort of American supper, so that's actually quite good for meeting. When we moved in, there was that, there was a barn dance, which was a PTA thing.... June ran the Brownies for a year or so.

Unless you positively opt out of doing things you tend to get roped in. Things like fêtes, for example – there's always requests for... can you bake a cake? Can you man this stall? Can you supply some plants for the plant stall? There's the

Produce Show every year, we both got involved with that. We've all won prizes. The last year I didn't get a prize personally, but the year before I got first for making a cake. Made a Swiss roll the morning of the show; literally took it along with about two minutes to spare before the close of the entry.

What is it about the New Forest that you and your family value most?

First and foremost, open space. Undeveloped land. The New Forest I think is important because it has a blend of different sorts of environment – trees, heaths and open fields – so it's the balance, the mixture. It isn't just an artificially created thing like a park. It's been around sufficiently long that there's a natural evolution that's taken place. So it's got some history, it's got things like the ponies, the cows and so on that can wander around freely. It's like the typical picture postcard thing, there is that uniqueness of character – the commoning, the whole management concept of the Forest. The Verderers even.

My view is that things like low-cost housing, while they are understandable requirements for those who cannot afford housing at the normal market value, that can't be a good long-term strategy. What you really need to do is to be able to fit in with the laws of supply and demand. The moment you try and tamper with them you get imbalances which generally cause more problems than they're worth. There are many aspects of Forest life which can create opportunities. Tourism is the obvious one. There are people locally who are providing bed and breakfast

The Forest pub scene, 1.

accommodation, so that is a form of employment. I think there are aspects of crafts that could be exploited a little more.

Eric, publican

Early morning: a pub on the edge of a Forest heath. There is the sound of a vacuum cleaner, chairs are upturned on tables – but there is no smell of stale tobacco or beer. In the bar there are sofas where you might expect benches or settles. Eric is in his thirties and speaks with a northern accent. It's a 300-year-old coaching inn so it's got all the character that you need, with nooks and crannies and beams. A general homely feeling.

What was this pub like when you first took over?

Well, dowdy. It was run down to a point where there wasn't any real interest in the place. There was a few locals came in now and again for their odd pint in the evening but no real atmosphere. You might go three or four hours in an evening and not serve a drink. Well, it was February. You weren't selling enough to pay for the electricity to light the place. That's what we've got to work against next winter. The summer trade here speaks for itself; were surrounded by campsites and caravan parks and so the people are here, out to enjoy themselves. It's the ideal pub for them, with a garden for the children and ventures outside, so we've got to cash in on that this first season, but

104

The Forest pub scene, 2.

then concentrate on building that winter trade up. To do what we intend doing is having special events each evening. Sunday night will be quiz night, Monday night darts night, Tuesday possibly ladies' darts, Wednesday a skittle evening, Thursdays we're going to have a 1930s night... people are invited to bring their own 78s in. We've got an old radiogram in the corner which works perfectly – it's got a lovely tone to it – and so we want to attract people out on Thursday nights for a Glenn Miller evening or a '20s or '30s or '40s – that sort of era, when we can couple it up with a nice supper menu.

Fridays and Saturdays will be busy anyway on the food because our reputation seems to be growing on the menu that we've put out. We've got a very New Foresty traditional feel to the menu, with venison, Hampshire tatie

A message in the sky, one hot day in 1998.

pots, casseroles and fish; because we're near the coast we specialize a lot in fresh fish.

We have brought in the 'Giant Frying Pan', which we hope to call 'Desperate Dan's Frying Pan'. We cook in that paellas, stir fries.... Although we have a traditional New Forest menu it doesn't stop us from having a Chinese night or a Japanese evening or a Taiwan evening. [The frying pan is] three foot in diameter and six inches deep and there's a handle which is two foot six long. It doesn't lend itself to tossing too many pancakes – it's made out of cast iron and weighs well over a hundredweight. We are going to weigh it and put it into a competition so people can guess what it weighs. If you do a stir fry in it or a paella, obviously people in the pub can see it being cooked from raw so they know it's absolutely fresh and if they didn't come in to eat and they see it being cooked, hopefully they'll find it pretty hard to resist.

How do your local customers view this change of style?

Well, initially it was with great trepidation because every time they came in they saw something different. Perhaps I would have put a settee in or some pictures, or painted a wall... it made the place not how they remembered it. Consequently a lot stayed away, but they've come back to see what I've done to the place and then have stayed. Eight years previous to our taking over, the landlord that took it over then had taken on a different proposition again. It was, from all reports, back another twenty years. It was really out of date, it was a spit and

sawdust place, it had a rough element in it, and he did more or less what we're doing now; tidying the place up, revamping it and sorting out the clientele to make it an easier and happier place to run.

How do you define a 'rough element'?

It's a group of people who would come into the pub and not be averse to causing problems, like fighting or swearing, generally not behaving themselves in a manner where you could accept a family. If it's a family-orientated pub, obviously we can't have.... There isn't a rough element in the pub at the moment – it's a smashing clientele – but there has been in the past – not necessarily from this area.

Ray, earth mover

A windy evening in June, with rough water on Hatchet Pond. I am visiting a house which obviously was once a council house. In the living room are two young people (in their twenties), one eating a snack, the other asleep in an armchair. Ray and I sit at the table. He has a thin, tough outdoor face. Before starting his own small business, he worked for a local agricultural engineer.

We paid £17,000 for one digger and £23,500 for the other, plus the VAT – we got the VAT back eventually. Touch wood, a month ago we made the last payment on the bigger one so they both belong to us now.... But you got that feeling that every month that man's stood there with his hand out for those payments on the digger, and you

A nursing home...

...converted from a 'big house'.

got to scrabble on, daylight to dark.

Bigger they are the easier they are to drive. The smaller ones, everything's manual; but as soon as you get up in size you get power-assisted this and power-assisted that and electronic on here... and a lot of it is of use. You sit in there every day and it's like a woman sat at a typewriter, she's looking out of the window going... with her fingers. And you sit there doing the same... you just got your hands on the levers.

Our biggest customer is these small sewage treatment plants we do for rest homes and pubs and hotels. [It's] just really a catchment tank at the end of the freefall drain runs – gravity drain runs – you have a catchment tank with two electric pumps in the bottom with macerators built into them that chew all the sewage up. They push it up a two-inch plastic pipe, up hill and down dale until you can pump it into a main sewer. We've pumped it as far as two miles for a rest home down at Lytchett Matravers, to get it out into the sewer. If anybody's got any sewage problems, if you can pump it and get it in the main sewer then it becomes the local authority's problem. Brian, with the bigger machine, goes round putting in actual sewage treatment plants – the drains run into a tank and then all the liquid goes through these treatment plants that are full of bacteria, and they pump air through it and.... They say that when it comes out the other end you could drink it but I don't think I'd be that... but it does clean it. Providing then you can let it run into a ditch – it's got to have a certain flow of water at all times – either a ditch or a river, they'll let you discharge it into a river.

Why do the new nursing homes have to have new sewage plants?

Usually it was a big, old country house, a well-to-do family that used to live in these big houses in the country. The existing sewage set-up was quite adequate for one family – mum, dad and perhaps two or three kids – it worked quite well. In those days there was no washing machines or dishwashers and three or four baths a day. Then the kids grow up and marry and move away and it goes back down to mum and dad again, living in this big house. Then perhaps they die and the children are settled wherever they've moved to and they don't want to come back to this big house, so it goes up for sale and somebody buys it for a rest home. And then all of a sudden there's twenty old people in there that have to be bathed every day and change the bedclothes every day and perhaps their clothes and... there's dishwashers going and two or three washing machines going – all day. The existing sewage set-up – just not built to cope with all that, it's just overworked.

This 'going green' thing, these environmentalists, they've done us a world of good. You've only got to get somebody complain to the council that somebody's drains are smelling and somebody's soon out there investigating and they've got to do something about it.

These houses you're talking about – would they be on the main sewage system?

No, they usually only got their own septic tank or cesspit. All that sort of thing relies on soak-aways; a septic tank usually just traps the solids inside the tank, which digest theirself and break down a lot and the liquid runs through. But when you get twenty old people living in one house and all this extra liquid going through, the soak-aways can't cope with it all. It waterlogs everywhere and floods all across.... We had a case down the road where there was a house up on some higher ground, changed to a rest home, and they were merrily doing whatever they had to do with all their dishwashers and that sort thing, and the woman down the road.... She probably lived fifty yards away down over the hill – she couldn't walk on her lawn in the summer. She had to stand on her lawn in wellingtons because all this water was waterlogging the field and coming all across her lawn. You wouldn't believe it. When it hangs around, then it goes all black like any stagnant water would – black, and stinks. I had to go up there and dig some investigatory holes and see what the problem was, and my digger stunk for a fortnight.

Stuart and Maria, at the village post office

A July evening. We are in the garden behind the post office and shop; there is a picnic table with the remains of a meal. Stuart and Maria are young middle-aged. Their children are playing further up the garden. Next door a neighbour noisily strims the garden.

Stuart:

We lived in Sussex and I worked for an airline in the cargo section, putting on all the stuff that goes underneath the aeroplanes in the hold. I was on the clerical side, supervising what was going on and what was coming off planes. I worked there for twenty years and it was time to make a move; I'd worked for a big company all these years and was a bit fed up with all the passing the buck and being told to carry out silly ideas, and unions. I very much wanted to do something on my own. The airline was a bit shaky so they were after getting rid of staff. I volunteered and we looked around for a completely different job and way of life. We were looking around at – definitely shops with post offices – we were looking in all various areas, but we found this place in the New Forest which suited all our needs.

Stuart at the entrance to his shop.

109

A village cottage.

The post office is solely run by me and one of my staff. The papers arrive here about quarter to six in the morning, after the milkman – the milkman arrives about half past three, so if it's a hot summer's day and you've left the window open you hear him. I'm up and down there by six but already nine times out of ten the milkman has arrived and the newspapers and magazines are outside waiting for me. My [news] boy comes out just before seven o'clock. He's got about forty houses to deliver to so I've got to get all of his newspapers and any magazines ready for him. Put the milk away, have a look what fruit and veg I require, because they come most days from a wholesaler in Southampton – they normally come about nine o'clock. I open my post office up at eight o'clock, so I get all the post office stuff out – the money, the postage stamps, all the various forms and books I might require. Rubbish – there's always rubbish from the newspapers, so whatever needs doing there because once a week the rubbish man comes. Wake the kids up, get their breakfast, cup of tea, breakfast for me, quick change, and by that time – hopefully – it's not yet eight o'clock.

At eight o'clock, there's three buses leave here within ten minutes taking people to work, big schoolchildren, small schoolchildren, so there's about thirty people outside – which is good for business – and about twenty mums, all wishing to buy bits and pieces. So by a quarter past eight you've quite often had about fifty to sixty people in. That is the main rush hour. Then you get a variety of – normally builders – between eight and nine, people who are just starting to travel to work, normally coming into the village. There's a few regulars who are going out but if there's quite a lot of work going on in the village they will stop off for their newspapers, pies, crisps. Then the postman comes. He's invariably got mail or stock or money for me, I need to get that put away. Then the woman who works in the shop, she comes in at nine o'clock. By that time there's been quite a lot happen. If the paper boy's not available, then I'm out on my bike delivering the papers.

After that it settles down into a pattern. Most of my work in the morning is in the post office. I've normally got a delivery of some sort, of cigarettes, sweets.... Man comes out with pies, man comes out with cheese, ham, cards, stationery. Groceries once a week, eggs once a week, frozen food once a week, ice cream man once a week – an amazing amount of people.

Do villagers use your shop as a meeting place?

Quite often, yes; especially the older people. They don't arrange to meet people but they do like to stay and have a chat, inside or outside. Sometimes you could be waiting ten minutes, quarter of an hour to serve somebody, they're just chatting away... it's nice. Sometimes it's quite comical.... Yesterday I had four ladies in and I decided that between them all they must have weighed about sixty or seventy stone. There was a big lady followed by a bigger lady followed by a bigger lady followed by a huge lady – and they were all in the shop. They all knew each other and they were all chatting away....

[The village is] spread out. All the population's on the east because the west is the Forest, and Main Road

Village living style.

probably goes on for about four miles, with population all the way down. Because it's not a typical village with a typical solid heart to it... it does go on and on. We've discussed class and we don't know quite how to define it.... There's definitely – if you're not snobby – there's definitely a lower class of people who live here. Quite a lot of them. Probably people that you could trace have lived within five miles for the last hundred years. And then there's a... I don't know... lower middle class?

Maria:
I absolutely hate dividing people up like that. I don't think it's anything to do with that. People just group themselves up according to their interest and background. I think the newcomers with children tend to make one cluster; the middle-aged people who are involved with the church and luncheon club and so on make another group. And then the people who've always lived here and their parents have lived here and parents before them, they tend to think of themselves.... I don't know if they do or they don't, but they tend to be another group who understand each other.

Stuart:
Yes. And then quite a few people who even since we've been here seem to have moved in and not particularly blended in at all. Either weekenders or people who just seem to use their houses for living in but not touching the village.... I may look and think, 'Who's that person?' I've not seen them in a year and they're not involved in any village interest, that they're just using their house – which is fair enough, if

that's what they want. A quiet place in the country, in the Forest.

There's a village fête – in fact that was last week – but there's a certain type of person that you won't see there, but you will see them in, say.... A month ago – there's two Sunday schools here and one of the Sunday schools had an outing to Weymouth and there were seventy people went on it from the section that, in the main, you wouldn't see at the village fête. We have often noticed occasions where, at what appear to be good fun for young families, invariably from a certain group you don't get anybody, probably because they're stereotyped into what they like and know. I'll tell you a good example – village pantomime. The village pantomime is over in the village hall, in the most central place which is used by everybody at various times. But when you come to the village pantomime you hardly see those people – whatever group you call them – the poorer people, you hardly see any of them.

CHAPTER 3

The Visitors

Caravans blending into the New Forest.

Caravans and cattle, Brockenhurst.

There now follow some conversations with tourists on the New Forest campsites.

Richard and Sheila, caravanners

I discovered Richard and Sheila one summer morning when the Forest was scented after recent rain. A neat caravan parked among the trees, with two bikes by the door.

Richard:

I commute, stand to work every day to town – coming back as well. The train is always like that. I live about the nearest commuting station but inevitably you stand on the train. I took it on late in life, thinking, well, it won't be long before I quit altogether – but how a young person could start to commute to his work spending an hour or two each journey – it's ridiculous. Complete waste of time.

Our caravan – it's fairly elderly, it's about ten years old now. It's quite a long one. It has a double bed at either end of it although there are only two of us – we usually leave one end made up as a bed and sit at the other end. It's got everything we need – it has running water, hot and cold. It has a heater. We have brought a television with us. At the moment we're hooked up to a mains supply. We also have gas for our oven and rings – Calor gas. We have 12-volt electric lights all round, plus fluorescent lighting over the kitchen part. The only objection we have to the whole thing is that the bathroom area is too small. The little wash basin in there drops down from the wall, but when you're sitting on the loo your nose is practically rubbing on the sink.

Where does the waste water go?

Sheila:
Containers underneath – and then we empty them.

Richard:
We have big, square containers which we carry on wheels.

And how do you get your fresh water?

Richard:
We have a thing called an aquaroll, which is a great big barrel on rubber rollers which we can roll to the water and fill up. Very clever indeed, the aquaroll. Some use them for waste water as well.... We always caravan now.

You've been coming to the New Forest for about fifteen years. Can you detect a New Forest accent now?

Cyclists on a forest track, Lyndhurst.

Hatchet Pond.

Erosion caused by pony trekking near Ringwood.

Richard:
No.

Sheila:
No. I can detect the Dorset very well, but not the New Forest. Perhaps the New Forest accent is very similar to Sussex and that's why I don't notice any different.

When I was here a few days ago I was talking to you about the difficulty the Commoners have buying property and about the threat to their way of life, running their animals on the Forest land. Had you been aware of those problems before then?

Richard:
I knew they did it, but that they have a problem, no. Except the obvious one that property is so pricey here because outsiders are moving in.

Gran and grandchildren, campers

It is the end of July, a warm afternoon. The small caravan is on a campsite, deep in woodland.

We're having four weeks altogether in the New Forest. We live in the New Forest, we really like it. We've got bikes but I'm sorry to say we've got punctures in two of them and we didn't bring any puncture outfit, so we can't go far. But we was intending to go right down to Bramshaw.

What do the kids do?

Oh, they got a swing thing up in the tree there. It was here when we come here. So they get on that and swing around. And they ride the bike, play water fights – buckets of water. They got soaked this morning. One starts to cry

A drift – ponies in the holding pen.

and the other one starts to fight [she laughs]. They love it. They come from Andover, so it's different for them to come out here. Tuesday, it was pouring down Tuesday. We'd just got our caravan in. I said, 'This is going to be a lovely holiday!' They played games – we got games for them in the caravan – played bingo, that's what we likes playing – we shout 'House!' and all. [She laughs.] Children really love that.

The squirrels, they attract us, all round our caravan. We think it's fantastic. The children sit for hours and watch them. If anybody says to me, 'Where can I go on holiday?' I say the New Forest. It's nice for the children, there's lots of things they can do and get about, can't they – they haven't got to be penned in. Like when they go to holidays at Butlins, they've got nothing really, they've got to be penned in.

An extended family in two caravans

Young woman:
When we go away in a caravan it's normally here, to the Forest.

Middle-aged man:
We love it, we come as often as we can. It's the free and easy life, the beautiful scenery, the change from the normal daily routine of living on a council estate.

Older woman:
We bird-watch, don't we and rabbit-watch. We had an owl yesterday. It came into the caravan and was on my son's knee.

Young woman:
Oh yes, we were here three weeks ago with that thunderstorm. We sat here

117

and watched it all come over. Lovely. We were sitting here at half past nine and we saw it all flashing in the distance and we said, 'Cor! Someone's having a hell of a storm!' Probably Bournemouth or somewhere. And it gradually got closer and we saw this sheet lightning with the forks coming down through it, behind that house. It was brilliant, brilliant. We were sitting here in our chairs watching it and it was right overhead and it was going well for about an hour before it actually rained. When it rained we went under the awning and watched it from there. It really did rain then.

[To one of the children] Was it frightening?

Child:
Only that big one.

Young woman:
One enormous great big bang – and they disappeared under the blankets, didn't you! And I even ran in from the awning. [She laughs.] We enjoyed that. That made our weekend. We thought we'd be flooded next morning but it drained really well, it was fine.

Older woman:
We like to get a site that don't allow dogs, but most of them do. When we're home we get a lot of trouble with other people's dogs... we're a little bit anti-dog. We get barking dogs and then we get mess from them and you have to be so careful where you walk, and that puts us right off.

The man who didn't like Sandy Balls

A man with his two daughters, aged eleven and six. It is now August and all the schools are on holiday.

Beaulieu Road pony sales.

118

Sandy Balls.

First time we came we went over to Sandy Balls caravan site, which is highly commercialized to my way of thinking. [Sandy Balls: A privately run campsite about three miles from the Forestry Commission site he finally chose. Sandy balls are little sandhills (so the brochure says).] This time I went to go to Sandy Balls, couldn't get on so we came here. They thoroughly enjoy it – so much to do. Went cycling yesterday, hired bikes. This morning pony trekking. Been down to Bournemouth, swimming – swimming pools and down the beach.

What do you like doing best?

Sit here and relax. It's just a nice break, so peaceful. The girls are happy playing. The [campers] down there, they were down last night, had a few beers, met them down the pub last night. Came back here, went up drinking coffee, and the kids playing cards. Total freedom, isn't it? You can go anywhere, do anything. This morning to go out on those ponies! Pony trekking – that was over at Godshill, near Sandy Balls. I thought I'd give the kids a treat. They go horse riding anyway at home but that's just in a field and they go round and round in circles. This was a totally different experience... I even joined in. I should think we must have done a seven-mile round circuit and they take you out right in the middle of it, not to the roads – you're up amongst the bracken and the tracks.

I don't agree with this bloke over here – no disrespect to him – he's got a luxury caravan, he's got a generator he plugs in at night.... That for me is getting away from what it's all about.

119

[This] is a basic little caravan – I've got gas and that's about it. That's all you need. Put the table down to make the bed, bunk bed up for the kids. It rained hard Tuesday night, threw it down. It was just a bit noisy on the roof – only aluminium.

An older couple from near Bath

A hot morning. The ponies are gathering under the trees further down the campsite and noisily mating.

Woman:
Every time I go out I say to you, don't I, I love it here. I've heard more people say that this is one place they'd like to live. They don't want to move anywhere else, but they would love to live in the Forest. It's beginning to get a little bit congested. Lyndhurst – all that heavy traffic going through Lyndhurst, I think that's a shame. It's such a pretty little place. Lymington, we went yesterday afternoon, we had an awful job to get parked. Today we went down to Calshot beach but there were so many wasps... and it was so hot.

Man:
First day we went down there, wife got bit – she had to go to the doctor's with it. Stuck it out three days. Today it was dreadful. You just couldn't eat your dinner; we had to come on back.

Woman:
We didn't get anything sweet out, we was frightened to. They were just swarming us, you know.
Man: Yes, soon as Sue got the orange squash out we had them, didn't we? Oh

my God!

Do the ponies cause you any trouble?

Oh, they have a go at our tent. Last time we come down they broke a guy rope; this time they broke the loop out of the guy rope ad split the tent – we had to sew that up.

Woman:
I think they could do with this 40mph speed limit round this part, though. We came through that part where they have got the speed restrictions up and I think they ought to have more of that. If you're travelling home on a dark night....

Man:
Specially when the mist is going across the road a bit, you got to be careful.

Woman:
The cars, they just overtake you. They can't possibly see properly.

Man:
Is there many get killed?

Woman:
There's no need for it. It's only because people are going too fast.

Man:
When we come here the first time there was a lot of ponies about here, in this patch alone. We went over to your sister's, didn't we, and your sister's husband said, when we was coming back – we wanted to get back before it got really too dark because of the ponies; he said they will lie down on a warm day, in the middle of the road at night. So

we was well warned and we've expected it ever since, so they're not much bother to us really. We just accept it.

Woman:
It's part of the Forest, isn't it?

Celia and Anna, long-term weekenders

An old cottage, one of a row, with a splendid view over the heath towards the Isle of Wight. Celia and Anna are sisters. We talk in their comfortable sitting room on a sunny weekend morning in September.

Anna:
There was a rope factory on this whole site and these cottages were the [rope] walk.

Celia:
The factory cottages. This is No. 1, Factory Cottage. They were eight back-to-back workers' cottages.

Anna:
The accommodation faced the Forest and the rope works were at the back.

When you drive down from London in the winter, are you travelling in the dark?

Celia:
We'd normally come on a Saturday morning.

Anna:
We go back in the dark all through the winter, which doesn't bother us very much. We do consciously try to avoid driving in the dark coming down because of being tired after a day at work in London....

Celia:
It's more relaxing to have an evening in London and then set off reasonably early on Saturday morning. We're usually down here by about quarter to eleven. We always used to do it but then we'd get down to a cold cottage. We both work rather hard and we were getting home from work, throwing our things in the car, getting in the car – and sitting in traffic. Seemed stupid. It was stressful and it spoilt the beginning of the weekend. Whereas we seem to find that almost every Saturday morning the weather is beautiful and we have a lovely drive out of London into the country.

One thing we do enjoy doing in the nice weather is going on the beach. We go down to Hordle, because we love the sea and we love beach life. Last summer we went several times. There's not a lot of time, really. But we're both of us getting nearer the time when we will be able to spend more time here. That's always there, at the end of the rainbow.

Is that the plan?

Oh yes, oh yes. And then we'll get absorbed into village life and do much, much more. There's not an awful lot that happens at weekends. We go to the Village Players and we go to the odd jumble sale, we go to as much as we can. And of course we see people in the shops – and when you asked me last time whether we ever saw any sign of being resented by the locals, we have never seen any sign of it, and we greet people in the shop as if we live here.

And we make use of things; we – or at least I – am a great blackberry picker and get all our kindling for lighting the fire from the Forest. Great one for doing that – go out with the wheelbarrow like an eccentric and fill it up and trundle it back here....

Anna:
[I've] been known to go out and pick up the horse manure, but we haven't done that for a few years. The autumn's lovely here....

Celia:
And winter is, too. A crisp, sunny winter day is simply gorgeous here. We're more inclined to go for a walk in the winter than we ever do in the summer.

Anna:
And we love our log fire. That is another something that, if we're sitting

in London during the winter, we actually look forward to.... Because that fire, when we fill it up with logs, that is amazingly good for us on Saturday nights in the winter; it's very therapeutic, no matter how dire everything is. Light a log fire.

Derek, campsite warden

Late September, and the rain sweeps across the heath. Near the little office-cum-shop I meet Derek, and to get out of the wet we talk in the cab of his Range Rover.

We open the week before Easter and we close the last Sunday in September. This year it was a very early start and the weather was atrocious. You see nobody, because they're either sitting in their caravans or they've gone out for the day. The caravan site looks absolutely dead, but there are sixty-odd

The scene near the sisters' cottage.

units on, a unit being a car and a caravan, a car and a tent, whatever. For a small, private campsite, that would be a lot of people, but for this size of campsite it is nothing at all and very easy to handle, especially mid-week. At this time of year, and early, you're out of school holidays, so it's mainly OAPs and people taking very late holidays. Bank holidays are a totally different thing. The whole Forest gets full, let alone the campsites. Just here, because we're north of everything, we're the last ones to fill up. The big campsites get filled on the Friday evening. When everywhere else is full and we're the only ones left open, everybody's being directed to us by the other campsites and the tourist information centre – even the policemen out on the roads. So on a Saturday we've got a queue right back to the road trying to get onto the campsite. And of course you get a tremendous variation of types of people in. You get the people coming out of London just out for the weekend – never been camping before in some cases, borrowed a tent. Having said that, we get very few problems here, maybe two or three incidents a year. For instance, last week, when it was all very quiet, we had a 'domestic'; a young couple fall out and instead of the usual thing like most of us – a few hours of silence between the two of you – the guy goes a little bit silly. starts doing silly things. So we have a little bit of a problem to sort out; so we sorted it out.

Were you here when the New Age travellers came to this part of the Forest?

Yes. It happened on a Thursday, which is my day off. We have relief wardens to cover for us and I came back in the middle of the afternoon and there's the travellers, or the hippies, parked right outside the gate, which completely ruins my day off. It went right through the weekend, from the Thursday at three o'clock until the following Monday at two o'clock, when they vacated the site. On the Thursday evening they left the entrance to the campsite and went down to Janesmoor Pond. There was ninety or a hundred vehicles – that's hard-core travellers. Then on the Friday and Saturday and Sunday nights they were joined by the part-time hippies out of the outlying areas. That's the youngsters that work all week but wanted to join the hippies for the big party that was being held in the evening – so then that at least doubled the ranks. They vacated at two o'clock in the afternoon on the Monday and they didn't give us one iota of trouble. They never set foot in the camp, they never tried to.... But of course I don't know this until after it's happened. I am virtually trying to keep awake for twenty-four hours a day. I can call on people to help me; the Forestry Commission are there and the police are there. But I just don't... or can't have these sort of people coming onto the campsite because they are not people who want to pay camping fees. And there was a risk of disease because of their dogs. The area had to be kept clear for the next two weeks.

How did the caravanners on the campsite react?

Well, some were a bit nervous at first. On the first night [the travellers] had a massive party. When these hippies had this party – I mean, they bring in musical equipment from miles around. The musicians were down from London. It's a highly organized thing. There was quite a bit of noise, but luckily for us the wind changed the next night so it took all the noise away from the campsite. But it went off without incident and we are now assured that it won't happen next year, so that's one little problem hopefully we've got rid of. They were given the use of the day visitors' toilet. They actually left the site quite clear – they put all their rubbish in black bags and stacked it. We went in and took it away and then did a litter-pick on the site and there was no more rubbish from them. It was maybe even less than a normal Sunday afternoon, because the general public can be very, very untidy.

It's now September, so presumably this site will close soon?

The campsite closes twelve o'clock Monday lunchtime. Everybody has to be off by then. We then do the clearing up and we will vacate the site on the Wednesday. What buildings are left are shuttered up and then that's it. All the wardens are the same; come the end of the season you're glad to get away from it. After Christmas you can't wait for the season to start again.

End of an era:
Peter, hunting kennelman

The hounds are baying in the kennels as I arrive. In Peter's cottage, we talk in an office-cum-living room. Hunting-green uniform is hanging on a wall. Peter is a youngish (thirty or forty-year-old) Forester.

I hunt the hounds. We've got two packs here, beagles and the buckhounds. Beagles hunt hares. We hunt deer, fallow deer. And the foxhounds are up Lyndhurst – three packs of hounds in the Forest. Buckhounds hunt Mondays and Fridays, foxhounds Tuesdays and Saturdays and the beagles Wednesdays and Saturdays. We start September, we hunt through September and stop in October because that's when the fallow deer are rutting; then we start again November and carry on through till April 1st. Foxhounds, they start in August and hunt straight through till April. Beagles are the same.

What's your daily routine?

I usually start about seven o'clock. Clear the yards up. Then I walk the hounds out – eighteen couple. We've got another kennelman here; he usually does the beagles, then we walk them out. This time of year we just go round the field with them, because they're hunting twice a week. Today the beagles were hunting so we sorted out what beagles they wanted to take, put the lame ones back and the old ones. Then we usually come in for breakfast. Then we had some phone calls – there was a pony knocked down at Norley Wood that was beside the road so they wanted that cleared up. I went and picked that up; then I went and picked a heifer up that had died of acorn poisoning. Brought them back. I had a phone call from [a stud farm] – they'd had to have their top stallion put down. At the minute we got so much flesh here I couldn't cope with it so I rung the

Hounds at work. (9C)

foxhounds and they dealt with that. What else have I done? Cleaned my boots, coats, ready for Friday. In a minute I shall feed the buckhounds. Usually by then the beagles are back so they got to be fed. We go through the beagles to see if there are any lame ones. By that time, it's usually dark. You nearly always get one or two lame ones come back. Usually it's gorse stuck in them, or they've took the skin off the pads. This time of the year tisn't so bad because the ground's got softer, but earlier on when it was hard, that's when you get most of your problems. Perhaps we lose a hound, and then you've got to go back and find it. Especially puppies – this time of year we've got a fair few puppies and they haven't usually got quite so much sense as the older hounds. [We] just go out there with horn and blow....

How do you train them to come to the sound of the horn?

We've always got enough old hounds here. As soon as you blow a horn, they come. And we couple the young ones to the old ones – two leather straps, put one on the puppy and one on the old hound, they're coupled together. They don't hunt like that, but when we're exercising or walking out that's what we do. When we meet, we always meet in the Forest on a particular keeper's beat. There's twelve keepers. When we get there in the morning, that Commission keeper's always there and he does what we call the harbouring – he goes and

125

New Forest deerhounds, early twentieth century. (9C)

selects what deer we got to hunt. Usually there's more than one deer, there's generally five or six, sometimes anything up to twenty. What we do, we draw out three, perhaps four couple of older hounds, they're called the tufters. We tuft the deer out with those three or four couple. When you first lay on the deer, the scent of that deer, it's cold. After that deer's been hunted for twenty minutes, half hour, his scent changes. As he gets warmer, his scent's different to a cold deer. Usually he goes away from the other deer – then we put the pack on, which is another six, seven couple.

If that deer runs back in with fresh deer, his scent to those hounds is different to a cold deer so they should be able to hunt that deer through the fresh ones. It doesn't always work. There's some hounds out there won't ever hunt a cold deer and if they do change, there's three or four couple

there'll always come back and tell me. Then we stop the others – it is usually the puppies – and we've got to find our hunted deer. It usually takes [the puppies] a good season before they know what they're doing. Our oldest [hound] would be nine year old now, I reckon. I've got one that doesn't like to be handled, he's a bit fierce. They're all different. For instance, if you want to worm them, there's some'll come straight up to you and you can put the tablet in their mouth and they'll take it. There's some, there's no way you can get it in; we've got to bribe them, put it in a bit of meat.

Some of the older ones are slower, but they're the ones that usually work it out in the end. If they haven't got a good brain on them they're no good. They got to think for theirself. A brain, a nose and a good voice. If a hound doesn't speak, he's no use to anybody. You do get that, they'll run mute. If he isn't speaking you don't know where he is, especially in the Forest. Sometimes, if you've checked, and you got a hound there that worked it out, where this deer's gone – and away he goes, and he's not speaking – the other hounds don't know where he's gone and he's away in front.... The older hounds just get jealous and they won't hunt. But if he's told them where that deer's gone, they're there, they're away.

Do the hounds look forward to a hunt?

Oh yes. They know which days we're going. They won't be fed. I shall feed them tonight, then they won't get fed tomorrow and they know when Friday comes round and they knows when Monday comes. They know in the morning when I go out there what we're going to do. When I walk them out and take them back in, there's some there that I don't take now because they're too old – but those that do go, they're always at the front of the queue, waiting to be drawed out. They know what day it is.

We have six weeks' to eight weeks' hound exercise before we start hunting, to get them fit. We usually go out early in the morning and our biggest problem's bloody dogs. Whichever way you go you run into dogs all over the place. Most of these people, they've heard all such terrible stories about hounds ripping dogs apart, so the first thing they do when they see a pack of hounds, they start hollering to their dog – which is the worst thing they can do. Straight away the hounds look up: 'What the hell's on?' If they said nothing they wouldn't take a blind bit of notice of the dog, but when they start hollering – you get some of these women, oh they hollers and screams – it's the worst thing they can do. You try to tell them to keep quiet, because a hound's the biggest coward in the world when it comes to another dog. They just go on by, especially if he looks a bit fierce. Wherever you go now, you got people hollering about at their dogs... five, six o'clock in the morning you can find them.

Even in remote parts of the Forest?

Oh yes. Well, there's no remote part really now, is there? Where we used to go and see nobody, now there's people everywhere.

Epilogue

I no longer live in Hampshire, but I returned to the Forest in the summer of 1998 to collect photographs for this book. Sadly, several of the contributors had died, which accounts for some of the gaps in the photographic record.

In the eight years which have elapsed since the first recordings were made, deer hunting has been stopped in the New Forest, which explains the photograph of the empty kennels. Where the hounds have gone I don't know. I believe they are unsuitable as pets and have probably been killed.

Every time I visit the Forest, an old rhyme keeps going round in my head. It was composed by 'Anon.' in the times when the common lands of England were being enclosed during the eighteenth and nineteenth centuries. Nothing of that sort is happening in 1998 of course, but yet I feel a great sense of loss, of deprivation, as if someone had stolen something from me. I cannot put this clearly into words, so I must let the unknown writer of this doggerel speak for me:

The law doth punish man or woman
That steals the goose from off the common;
But lets the greater felon loose
That steals the common from the goose.

Empty deerhound kennels.